DISCO FRITO

Peregrine Smith Books
Salt Lake City

RICHARD ELMAN

DISCO FRITO

First edition

90 89 88   3 2 1

Copyright © 1988 by Richard Elman

Published by Gibbs Smith, Publisher, P.O. Box 667, Layton, Utah 84041

Design by Formaz

Printed and bound in the United States of America

**Library of Congress
Cataloging-in-Publication Data**

Elman, Richard M.
   Disco frito/Richard Elman.
   p.   cm.
   ISBN 0-87905-289-9
   1. Nicaragua—Fiction. I. Title.
PS3555.L628D5   1988
813'.54—dc19   88-5425

DEDICATION

To the enduring people of Central America, to my
friends and comrades; for Margaret, Alice, Buzz, Nick,
and Ellen; to the memory of Peter Martin, bookseller
and friend to writers.

CONTENTS

Acknowledgments ix

Preface xi

PART 1

Béisbol (1978) 3

After a Long Spell in Chad (1981) 8

When They Killed "Macho Negro" (1979) 14

Chocolate (1981) 20

At Peñas Blancas (1981) 21

Weak Tambourines (1979) 23

Clandestines (1981) 28

Little Sharks (1981) 35

Two of Rik's After Dinner Stories (1984) 43

Café (1981) 46

Sucking Chest Wounds (1978) 49

In Tegucigalpa (1987) 54

Some Elves for the Shoemaker (1984) 57

The Secret Admirers (1979) 63

Marital Difficulties (1984) 67

The Anvil of the Times (1984) 69

On Credit (1981). 73

PART 2

In Tipitapa (1979) 87

Nicaragua and the Jewish Problem (1981) 89

Do You See Any Porters Anywhere? (1984) 93

Turnabout (1984) 97

Managua 4:30 P.M. (1978) 100

A Brief Interview (León) (1981) 108

Lillian (1982) 109

Dinner Out (1981) 114
In What They Used to Call Vietnam (1983) 115
The House Watcher (1981) 119
Don't Turn Right (1984) 128
Near the Campo de Marzo (1979) 134
The Old Woman's Stories (1981) 137
The Old Man's Stories (1979) 138
The Gulf of Fonseca (1981) 140
Loving Strangers (1984) 146
An Alleyway in León (1978) 148
Losing Parts (1984) 151
Prudhomme's Story (1984). 154
Rolex (1981) 157
Marco in Vermont (1984) 160
With Bravo in Rivas (1979) 173
Palmerolla (1983) 176
Alberto y Sylvia (1986) 180

PART III

Calamity 193
Hymie (1987) 194
Froylan Turcios Was a Long Time Ago (1987) ... 201

ACKNOWLEDGMENTS

Some of these stories have appeared in magazines and newspapers previously: "Béisbol" in the *Albuquerque Journal Magazine*, October 1985; "After a Long Spell in Chad," "Chocolate," "Café," "Marital Difficulties," and "Near the Campo de Marzo" in *Witness*, vol. 1, no. 4, Winter 1987; "Little Sharks" in *Antaeus*, Spring 1988; "The Secret Admirers" in *The Boston Review*, Fall 1987; "The Anvil of the Times" and "Turnabout" in the special fiction issue of the *Michigan Quarterly*, Fall 1987, vol. 1, edited by Nicholas Delbanco; "Clandestines" in the *Texas Review*, Fall 1987; and "An Alleyway in León" in the *Arizona Daily Star*, 1985.

I want to thank Gene McGarr of Venice, California, who underwrote one of my many trips to Central America.

PREFACE

Disco Frito is a work of fiction. Some of these stories were told to me and, perforce, became fiction in the act of retelling them. Some happened to me or my friends, and when I think of them again they are as fiction.

Fiction is one of the metaphors we have for experience. Except for certain public and historic figures mentioned herein, all the characters in this collection are fictional, including the principal narrator, Rik. Any resemblance to persons living or dead is strictly a coincidence.

The title *Disco Frito (Fried Disco)* comes about as a result of an incident that took place in 1978. In early September the FSLN firebombed the Frisco Disco, a popular middle-class disco owned by a Somoza crony. It was destroyed without loss of life. Afterwords the FSLN distributed a broadside which boasted: "*Ahorita Frisco Disco es Disco Frito (Now Frisco Disco is the Fried Disco)*."

"... Somozas from San Marcos,
Moncadas from Masatepe,
Sandinos from Niquinohomo.
All people from the same central
plain, no more than twenty kilo-
meters separating one and the
other. . . ."

Cesar Augustín Sandino to José Roman, his
would-be biographer, 1933

PART 1

BÉISBOL (1978)

Just below Barrio Quinta Nina, in some fields bordering
Lake Managua, I used to watch the teen-age kids playing
béisbol. They were prodigious athletes: though their curve
balls hung in the wind and they often had to run uphill to
reach first base, their energies never flagged. From hovels
of cardboard and scrap wood, where lives were poisoned
with the chemic greases and ordures of lakeside sewage,
they emerged during the late afternoons to disport themselves in club satins and neon-colored pin stripes: caps the
hue of papaya flesh or tomatoes; genuine spiked black
shoes on the feet of boys who usually went barefooted.

Everybody in the neighborhood took *béisbol* very seri-
ously, and some made it a habit of the spirit, something as
Nica to them as all the exotic colors in Ruben Dario's
poetry. They had newspaper knowledge of the big leagues
in El Norte, were adept at the various major league styles.
This one hit like Clemente or onehanded flies like a young
Willie Mays. They knew how to simulate Mike Marshall's
screwball overhand pitch and they took hook slides in
those fields of manure paddies and debris. Some even had
the looks of future standouts like Denny Martinez. But
they used balls as wilted as ragged vegetables from the
Central Market; and their bats pinched hands when they
connected with the ball.

The small knots of younger kids who stood by as a
cheering section seemed to enjoy the games almost as
much as the players. They shouted pet names, jeered all
errors. Nearby the women of the *barrio* washed clothes in
concrete troughs; and the grown men drank beer and raw
cane brandy and cleaned their weapons (for the Guard
might be coming at any time, even in the middle of the
night, to look for weapons). The scene looked as tranquil
as some mid-American meadow in late July: picnicking
campesinos, women attending to chores, boys playing ball—

except that when the games were over all the boys disappeared. They literally went underground, into an abandoned storm sewer along the lakeshore, where they fabricated contact bombs and mortar pipes. At night, with thoughts of Clemente and Martinez still in their heads, they sneaked out to take part in actions or to scribble graffiti on municipal walls against the dictatorship and its hated gringo friends.

I can only remember the name of one team from that Little Summer of 1978. *Quenipes*. They were all quite small, wore flashy green uniforms, garish with orange pin stripes as representations of these tart grapelike fruits. Caps shaped like melon ends. All of one month of summer I watched those midget champions cavort and then disappear, perhaps to die. Or they'd arrive without their usual first baseman, with bandaged legs and brows. Once they played a team of grown men from the nearby *barrio* of Vietnam and were swamped with homers, but every grounder hit to the infield was scooped up and thrown out by agile hands.

It was right about then that the first openly fought battles between the rebels and the Guard took place. I had business elsewhere, saw much that still haunts me. That Sandinista campaign of August–September 1978, though ultimately defeated, brought many of the cities to rubble. When I returned to Quinta Nina in late September, guardsmen in jeeps patrolled every street corner. I was a little reluctant to show my press credentials. The game was still in progress, though: *Quenipes* disporting themselves against a team of Creole mulattos from the East Coast who'd been transplanted to a nearby *barrio* and were thought to be politically reliable by the functionaries. They all had very large hands and feet and powerful hams, and I noticed their pitcher was easily overpowering *Quenipe* batters with his heavy fastballs.

4

After some time I also was aware my team was made up almost entirely of replacements. They wore the same uniforms with the same nicknames sewn across their chests, but these were definitely not the same players, not the same Oscar and Pepi and German I'd watched once before.

Then I also noticed the two plainclothes men from the paramilitaries who were spectating the game, each with an Uzi machine pistol on a sling dangling from his hand. This new game was being staged more for their benefit, I observed, than for the benefit of the players. I stayed around to watch.

My team was behind 5-to-1 by the time I came along. They barely swung their bats at incoming balls. Aside from an occasional walk to their littlest boys, they went down in order.

In the fifth inning, contact bombs exploded down lakeside near the big white Bank of America building. In the silence between bursts, men and boys stood about wondering what was about to happen next, and then abruptly they fled from one another and left me standing in an almost empty field.

A large pile of old bats had been left behind, along with somebody's spiked shoes. Nearby some women herded pigs. I started toward them but was stopped by the noise of more automatic rifle fire that seemed to trip my feet from under me. Some fifty feet away, two young women were still laying out a wash.

"The cathedral can have our relics," said one.

"The soldiers won't be coming now," the other said. "They have too much to do in Managua."

Night would soon be coming on, so I got up again, despite my fears, and loped toward the center of the *barrio*. At the first checkpoint I was stopped by a handsome Guard lieutenant who looked a lot like one of the boys who pose for Salem ads in the Latin countries: brown but clean cut. He wore U.S.-issue waterproof boots. When I found my papers and showed them to him, he seemed easily satisfied but asked, just to make talk, what I was doing in Quinta Nina. Lamely I said I'd come to watch a baseball game.

The lieutenant seemed awfully pleased with me. "*Hermano,* you can't see better *béisbol* anywhere in the world," he said. "Not even in Cuba. There are Nicaraguans in the big leagues. But, of course, the best players are in León—not here in Managua, but in León."

"I like their spirits," I insisted.

"You gringos always make that mistake," he pointed out, in a kind of Spanglais, for my benefit. "You buy the worst hammocks and you watch the worst *béisbol;* you are always looking for true grit in a greased pig."

When I asked if I could go now he seemed reluctant to dismiss me.

"If you want to see a pitcher," my new guide said, "you should see Caballo Negro of Number One León. He's old now, but once he struck out the entire Yankee lineup in order."

Then it suddenly went dark and the lieutenant told his squad to take cover. He also informed me he would drive me out to the main highway.

Thinking we would talk more *béisbol,* I got into the front seat with him. As soon as we were on the move, the lieutenant assured me he had very little use for the current state of affairs, or old Somoza and his whores. He was learning English "plain as the smile on your face," and he wanted to go back to school in the States to study sociology at UC Berkeley. He wished above all to be a "humane" penologist, or teach penology at a university. He could read Talcott Parsons, but he was just not a "Red." He said, "I am a compassionate person."

I told Lt. Martinez that, if I knew his address, when I got back to the States I would send him some college catalogs so he could make intelligent choices. Or I would just send the materials to Lt. Raoul Martinez at the Army Base, Campo de Marzo, Managua.

We'd reached the highway. "I would like the States, I know it," he said, "as I am sure you can tell."

"I'm sure."

"Bird in hand," he said, sticking out his hand. We shook, and then I left him there.

I know he didn't die in the fighting; I've checked the lists. So perhaps he's serving even now as a Contra for the CIA and "humane" penology or is in exile in Miami touting Nicaraguan baseball, telling his *mano* brothers in exile how he would someday like to translate Talcott Parsons into Spanish.

As for those Nicaraguan "boys of summer," many died fighting in the streets of Managua, Estelí and Matagalpa. Some are minor bureaucrats of the new regime. Some married, some went abroad to join the Contras or remain uninvolved, draft dodgers in Miami, Houston or San José, Costa Rica.

Baseball is played as much as ever in Nicaragua.

The warm tropical nights flow through the loins of all of us, even in our sleep, and the next morning we are all just a little older and feebler. ●

AFTER A LONG SPELL IN CHAD (1981)

In Managua one evening at the Momotombo bar, formerly a brothel, now a "club" for intellectuals in the government, I meet my old friend, Prudhomme from AFP (the French news agency). I've been going back and forth between Managua, New York, and Tegoo. He's just back in Managua after a long spell in Chad.

Polarities attract, as the French say: Prudhomme's English is OK, but he prefers to speak Spanish poorly, as I do. "We have to practice," he insists.

I ask what it was like being in Africa again.

"Better for a woman than a man," he says. "The men are tall and lithe, like animals. The women are ugly and they all smell. Never take baths. Ugly, passive little things."

"I'm very sorry to hear you say that Prudhomme, but I fail to see the significance."

"It doesn't matter. I refuse to be lonely *anywhere* anymore."

He's a slim man with a big mustache, as in certain Belle Epoque pornographic illustrations, but he's a fine reporter. I've heard him dictate extempore to Paris without notes over the telephone after a battle, in perfectly symmetrical Alexandrines. And he has experience, and a courage I lack: he was in Vietnam when France fought there, and in Algeria. He landed at Suez with the British and French.

Every sort of social upset where people resort to firearms is Prudhomme's *metier*. He's terrified of the local snakes and has a rotten stomach from various indigenous cuisines. "One man's poison is another man's poison, too," he always says, as though to justify his habits.

"Are there any good-looking women left in Managua?" he asks me now suddenly.

"They've all been commandeered by Party officials," I point out. "In fact some of them are Party officials."

"It's always that way." He swears. "The women get up off their backs and try to run things, and you and I miss out because the first thing they ban is the state-protected brothels where they once worked."

Prudhomme orders two Rum Flors with ice. "Why are we here now?" he shrugs. "What's the story?"

"Ortega says the U.S. will invade."

"What does the U.S. say?" he demands.

"They say the Contras can do the job without them."

"Then they are afraid of casualties," he points out, "but will probably invade anyway, as a last resort. The Contra can't do anything without them and Americans are the least trustworthy people in the world."

I've always known Prudhomme disliked *gringos,* but I never knew precisely why. Was it some form of admiration which could only be expressed negatively? I ask him now why.

Prudhomme twists his mustache and bares his teeth. "It's very simple, almost childish I suppose. The way you treat your friends is worse than enemies. Somoza was your friend all these years, and then you belly up him when he was desperate for a friend and the same is true of the Shah. You have such violent loves and hates, your public opinion. You provide and then you drop into the lake. So now you hate these callow Marxists but it was you who put them into power, no? After the fall?"

"Not me personally," I add.

"How like an American you are," he says. "Well, if we're here, we ought to make the most of it. Let's go see the President's wife. She likes a good gossip."

We finish our drinks and walk in darkness toward the brightly lit guard towers of Ortega's residence. Sentries are posted along the retaining walls under arc lights as bright as camera flashes. I wonder how it must be to try to sleep in such an atmosphere.

"War is *merde,*" Prudhomme boasts. "I scrape it off my boots."

He's sort of famous, so he has no trouble getting the officer of the Guards to admit us to the public rooms in the official residence.

A reception for some visiting Africans is in progress. The Chief of State looks small and feral, frail, surrounded by so many large black Africans. He looks like a little sleepy-eyed clerk, an accountant, with a mustache that's trim, though twitchy.

Prudhomme says, "Revolutions are loud. Do you notice?"

A tray falls somewhere.

The President and the foremost African diplomat embrace. Light scatters of applause. The pop of a soda bottle.

Ortega's wife talks to a swarthy soldier in custom-tailored fatigues and a forager cap. She's tall and dark, quite as I remember her, and svelte, with dark lustrous hair and a face heavily pocked, like fine ostrich leather.

Prudhomme pushes us into line to be greeted.

Rosario says, "When Langhorne Motley was their ambassador here all he wanted was the girls."

"That's the best I ever heard about your diplomats," Prudhomme says to me.

He adds, "Belly up for Langhorne means with a girl on top, jig jig jig."

A servant in a white jacket offers me a fish stick.

I recognize him. He is one of the boys who fought in Estelí.

Prudhomme says, "I wouldn't eat that if I were you." He grabs a couple.

The President's wife comes forward to greet us. The air feels refrigerated, smells of ozone.

"I am enchanted once again naturally," she tells Prudhomme, in French. As she reaches for his hand, she lifts her dark heavy eyebrows at me. Sultry like Theda Bara.

"I suppose you know," I say, "I am not a friend. Though not an enemy either."

"Have another fish stick," Rosario says.

Prudhomme says, "They have the same fish sticks in Chad and it's much hotter there."

I make a joke. "But these come from fishing in more troubled waters."

"Paul Simon—I think I love Paul Simon," says a pretty young Nicaraguan woman behind us, who must have overheard.

Prudhomme introduces himself by turning his back to Rosario and me.

Rosario is staring at me in such a cool, appraising way it's hard to tell what, if anything, is on her mind or what she has to say. Her hair reminds me of ice cream the color of coal I once had in Cadiz, Ohio, during the annual coal festival. I am tongue-tied by recollections of Rosario, too, in 1978.

Another *muchacho* in a white coat steps in front of us with a plate of meatballs.

"Do I know you from somewhere?" she asks me suddenly.

"1978 . . . September . . . the Writer's Club next door to the Butterfly brothel."

She laughs. "We travelled to Matagalpa together."

"And Chinandega," I recall. "There were demonstrations."

"You were very scared," she adds, as though to dismiss me. "Well so was I."

"Surely," I tell her.

11

Neither of us reaches for a meatball.

The young man says, "At your orders," before moving on.

Rosario says, "Different times different manners. Surely."

"Surely," I echo her again. *"Seguro."*

We bow at each other, with almost oriental politeness are dismissed by each other's eyes. I'm looking for Prudhomme once more, but he's just left the reception with a new lady friend.

A blond German in expensive sports clothes asks me if I'm detained in Managua.

He's from the East; I can tell by his spongy-soled shoes. I don't wish to be rude but I have very little more to say.

"You're American," he insists.

"Absolutely," I say, "like claymore mines, and apple pie."

"I see."

I start for the exit.

Night beyond the presidential complex is a tattered brocade of windowless houses and glowing cigarettes. The city seems at peace, at rest inside a countryside still at war. I almost stumble against the monument mound of one who fell in 1979, and, as I right myself, I know I'm hungry. *"Presente,"* I whisper into the darkness. "Here am I."

I know a man with whiskey and another with a VCR and first-run movies from Europe and Hollywood.

A man who rents hang gliders to bored journalists, if you pay in dollars.

Strange how the dollar has become more important than ever in Nicaragua since the Revolution.

A friend says, *"Cordobas* are cheaper than real toilet paper."

All of Managua is a deep inquietude, impenetrable, a pit of darkness overlooked by the Intercontinental Hotel pyramid and some adjacent restaurants.

I start walking toward the light, so distant and misleading, not half so attractive up close as it seems walking toward it in the darkness.

"Noches tropicales de Centro América."

Somewhere in the hills near Tiscapa a shot reverberates, and then another, then silence. Could be an anxious guard, or worse.

I stumble on some rubble. City of darkness, of silence, and sudden shots . . . City of sudden cries . . .

I quicken my steps. ●

WHEN THEY KILLED
"MACHO NEGRO"
(1979)

[When this story was told to me by an American photojournalist of
Tunisian origin, who often worked with Prudhomme on 'sendups' for
the French press, we were in La Ceiba, Honduras, in a bar called Sea
View. It was a rainy night and as soon as the rain stopped we were
expecting to fly to Roatan. Naythan Amer said, "Before Central America
I never felt afraid. Now I don't even like to fly when it rains."

Subsequent to his work in Central America, Amer quit photojournal-
ism after a colleague and countryman was killed in a cross fire in El
Salvador. He now does only "art photography" in French Polynesia.]

We were driving back to Managua after the execution of
"Macho Negro" in Masaya when we both started
jabbering.

"The rose, the rose," Prudhomme said. "Black mules
come and go . . . and lovely is the rose."

"There's one less mule in Spanish Harlem," I chanted
back.

He was flat out laughing. Though I didn't think I was
that funny, he couldn't seem to control his paroxysms.

I drove. Had to expel air, words. Tapping my foot
against the gas pedal and brake.

"Macho Negro this time did not make ceremonies to
stand on, no?" he demanded of me, the car, the still noon,
the battered, pitted landscape.

He suppressed another giggle with his fist.

"You mean standard ceremonies?" I asked. "Or stand on
ceremony?"

"Anyway," he said. "The bum is for sure dead."

"Dead at last, dead at last," we shouted back as the wind-
shield in front of us rattled. "Great God Almighty he be
dead at last."

"Macho Negro" was huge, a black creole from the East Coast in a country of smallish men, with a broad flat sullen face, oriental eyes. Our favorite nemesis always wore two magnum pistols stuck in the webbed belt of his bloused green fatigue trousers, a green garrison cap with a black metal skull for insignia. The only time I ever heard him speak in his loud raw Creole English was to threaten or say something obscene.

Once, when I asked directions from him in front of the Guard cuartel in Masaya, he told me, "I eat shit your grandmother."

Led by his capturers out of a shed into the back yard of a private house in Masaya, the pro-Yankee Macho Negro stared, without a blindfold, beside a coffee bush at his firing squad, the local block committee. His eyes were already glassy, dead, no different than they'd ever seemed to me.

"Now you must do it," he said without a word of argument or acrimony, a dare collapsing in his blood, his body torn apart by bullets. He'd been the number one rapist and murderer in Masaya, a sergeant, an extortionist, "unredeemable," in the words of a local magistrate, and very gung-ho. Before the new junta could pass its edict against capital punishment, local vigilantes were given permission to execute this monster. On impact, his glance chewed at our faces when he stumbled.

He'd been found lala crazy and cowering among the refugees at the Red Cross, legs done up in fake bandages as though he'd been crippled. Apprehended, "Macho Negro" did not struggle. He told the Sandinistas, "You will only be doing what I would have done."

His face a large flat black metal penny.

On such a hot overcast day, the beginning of a rainy spell, our silliness did us both some good. One more sensible killing wasn't making us feel better.

Quite close to the Plaza España we came upon a road-block. Young Sandinistas, after ousting a platoon of the Guard, were now busy acting as traffic police by checking on peoples' credentials before allowing them to pass into the capital.

The car had a tendency to stall in neutral, so I kept revving its motor as we waited to be checked out.

At last, we were passed up to a beardless youth in a maroon raw silk dinner jacket with darker satin lapels, cutoff jeans, a baseball cap advertising Bama Feeds, who told me not to waste precious gasoline by behaving like a *cabrone*. He asked to see our credentials.

Prudhomme had a French diplomatic passport as well as credentials from AFP, and he had me pass them through the window along with my police shields from New York, my Tunisian passport, an Avis card, and a tiny laminated letter from my editor.

The youth studied everything closely, with the unmantled ignorance of the illiterate, while car horns were blaring behind us, and then he glanced at the car's front fender, which looked a bit like a colander, and passed them all back again, and said, "Where have you just come from?"

"Masaya City," I replied.

He asked, "It's permitted?"

"Only to attend executions." Prudhomme began to laugh again.

The lad seemed edgy, unused to teasing. He started to point his weapon.

"Hola," Prudhomme said. "We're not rapists."

"Don't make fun of Sandinist power," the boy gravely said, as he passed us forward.

Less than two miles down the same highway we passed another checkpoint, and were asked to stop once again for questioning by a young woman with an angelic round cast to her dark face. She wore blousy brown-on-yellow leopard-spotted combat fatigues, a red beret, and had soft brown eyes, heavy lips, carried a Galil. "Some elements are looting," she explained. When I said we were coming from the execution of the dreaded "Macho Negro," the young woman replied with a slogan: "This is a revolution of love *mano*."

Prudhomme surely must have touched a sore tooth with his tongue for he winced: "Who shot you full of Novocaine, sister? Where do you learn such things?"

"It's being said even by priests," she replied. Her weapon jiggled; it looked as if it hadn't been cleaned in some time, and when she drew it down to her side with a glum look, that response still seemed to rely more on the touch of her trigger finger than on any courtesy or understanding.

Prudhomme said, "Our friend here has VCRs between his eyes. Would you like to witness an act of love? He could make it play back for you."

"Such things are understandable," she replied. "But the transnational press and the CIA always look for slanders, as you must know."

"When you asked us to make *fotos* of your friends it wasn't slander," I put in. "People are so fearful suddenly."

"It's just this Yankee I fear," she said, pointing her weapon toward Prudhomme. "For you I have no feeling, one way or the other."

She waved us on once more, and now we were both unhappy with our bumptiousness as we passed burial crews at work. Gunny sacks of ash and bones of the hastily cremated dead were being carried back to where they'd fallen and reburied by parties of their weary comrades. I thought of gardeners in the New York suburbs submerging the burlap-covered roots of cherry and magnolia.

I saw other armed kids who hadn't been a part of any of this a month earlier patrolling the streets. We passed a Mercedes billboard plastered over with larger-than-life faces of Fonseca and Sandino and, I think, Mayorga, and

announcements of forthcoming movies from Senegal and
Zimbabwe.

I told Prudhomme, "We could write, 'Macho Negro
woke up dead, thus an element of self restraint was added
to his habitual barbarism.' "

"This man deserved no obituary," he replied. "None at
all!"

I think even then we were both reflecting on the dead
sergeant's most infamous act: a murder by execution of six
teenagers in a cornfield near Nyarit. They'd been blind-
folded, hands tied behind their backs. Suspects executed, in
the words of the government tabloid, by unknown persons for unknown reasons.

We drove toward the new government house to check
our press releases. "I wonder if we really should write the
story of Macho Negro," Prudhomme was saying. "It's just
a sidebar. Hardly pivotal."

"He who lives by the bullet to the head," I reminded
him.

When that raggedy band of executioners were posi-
tioned, the Sandinist in charge asked Macho Negro what
he had to say before dying. He replied, "I was a soldier.
This was war."

The volley spun his great body half about, and then it
reeled, and sagged.

A few moments later one executioner asked
Prudhomme for a Marlboro. He told us, "Macho Negro
sometimes liked a Claro Fino but rarely cigarettes. Flor
Nica Naturales, you know."

Now Prudhomme said, "He had nothing to defend, no
honor. A shrug . . . and I thought a little smirk."

"He was totally frightened," I put in, "don't fool
yourself."

"How could you tell?"

"So," Prudhomme added, a moment later. "No more executions, so this one eventually must seem much less awesome than it really was."

"They've really promised," I said.

That evening at the hotel we read about the execution of common prostitutes in Iran and about Commander Bravo's last-ditch stand near Rivas against Pastora's forces, that the Guard, who'd all fled to Honduras, were even now being recruited by la CIA to fight as Contras, as they later came to be called. Prudhomme said, "More, more, and more to come."

It was only a couple of days after the victory, as I recall, and the man who told the latter piece of bad news was a Cuban journalist from EFA everybody called "the duck."

Just because liars like "el Pato" talk a lot, they have been known to tell the truth, as often as not. ●

CHOCOLATE (1981)

Some ammunition looks like things you can eat.

Some 30-millimeter cartridges look like fancy chocolates wrapped in foil, and there's a certain French rocket marketed throughout Central America which resembles a supermarket avocado: same dark green oval with a pebbly skin.

There's an Israeli assault rifle called the Galil I mistook at first for licorice rods.

I guess it's still pretty hard for me to accept people carry these things around if they don't intend to eat them or offer them to others. I always go out into the field loaded with chocolate bars and water. If they made a bandoleer wide enough to hold a chocolate bar, I'd arm it with 50-millimeter Droste bittersweets.

My friend Armando is originally from San Francisco. He lost part of his foot in 1978 and limps a little. Now he's political officer with the troops, dirty work. He eats a lot of my chocolates.

He says, "Ghirardelli's is sweeter. But this one has the taste explosion."

I say, "Acts like a bangalore torpedo on cavities and diseased gums."

"We're walking through the *barrio* Sutiava of León, where Armando buys me lunch. He's brown and in the sun his face seems to pucker.

Suddenly he turns toward me in the sun: "When I see bullets they make me happy. I know it's not right, but there were times in the mountains we didn't have any. I like to hold them in my hands and clink them sometimes."

I say, "Do you like the smell of cordite?"

"No," he rubs his face with the flat of his palm. "It makes my nose all sore. It makes me cry." ●

AT PEÑAS BLANCAS (1981)

The trailer truck parked sideways in front of the Nicaraguan customs post at Peñas Blancas leaks brake fluid and when we come alongside we see the cab ripped apart by 50-caliber machine-gun fire. A small pool of blood clots beneath the running boards; the cab's empty.

A militiaman in the shack at the border warns us against going any further. "Too much *tiroteos* today," he explains. "*Malditos Contras.* With a truck full of plastic. Better you go through elsewhere."

It's chilling to think we've almost parked next to a bomb. We back away as fast as we can until there's no place else to go, so we roll further backwards and park alongside a café and go inside.

The only other guest is a Sandinista officer of Customs in fitted green fatigues. He's sipping a cacao in a large wooden gourd. When he sees us he stops and calls out, "Do you see what your Ronald McDonald is doing to Nicaragua?"

I guess it's not too hard to tell we're from the North. I have no wish to defend my government, and no desire to hear it attacked. Prudhomme speaks in heavily accented English to prove the *comandante* in part wrong: "If these were Contras weren't they going in the wrong direction?" he demands. "Are they blowing up Costa Rica?"

"They wished to blow up the entire garrison here at the border," the *comandante* explains, "to make an incident."

He snaps his fingers at the waitress and orders white rum all around. "It's good for the nerves," he explains, "though crude."

"There were ten in the truck. Three in the cab died right away," he points out. "The other seven are still in the jungle."

"Probably they won't be back," said Prudhomme.

So just then the shooting waps at us again: light caliber carbines, I judge, plus the occasional explosion of a frag grenade.

I'm under the table. Prudhomme peers out a corner of the window. A bullet nicks the sill and he dives down next to the *comandante* who is cursing, *"Pendejos."*

He won't or can't get up, for his leg is jammed inside the legs of a chair. I see blood. "Are you hit?" I call out to Prudhomme.

"Of course," he says. "Spattered is more like it. Our officer friend has a fragment in his arm. Nothing serious, he just bleeds a lot, and we have nothing for a tourniquet. It seems . . ."

There's a final burst of small arms fire and then it all stops and darkness comes on, heavy and swift. The small surviving band of Contras has set up a diversion and made their way across the border. Prudhomme removes one of his long socks to tie the blood on the *comandante's* arm.

Outside the door we hear heavy footsteps. A patrol enters, armed *cap-à-pie*. Seeing the wounded man, the officer in charge says, "We'll take him back with us to Rivas."

"What about the damned truck?" Prudhomme asks.

"We looked inside," the leader explains. "There was nothing but hides, and a couple of dead calves. Such materials are contraband."

Prudhomme and I travel back in our car in convoy with the Sandinists ahead of us in their half-track. When we come to Rivas we drive right on, through darkness, the furthest dark hills seeming to erupt now and then with the sparks and flames of volcanoes.●

WEAK TAMBOURINES (1979)

The evening before a battle is worse than the battle.

We were off at dawn to Estelí to get there before the Guardia encircled the town and began the massacres.

Though it was past eleven, I could not sleep, so I went down to the bar for another nightcap.

The barman, whom we called Willy Mays because he was black and one-handed the preparation of drinks with great agility, asked if I had a "cat's skull."

"The opposite," I explained. "Too many chemicals, too much adrenalin in my system."

"If I had a hangover," I said, "I would just let sleep catch up to me."

"As you say." He poured me brown rum and whispered across the bar that one of the Sandinistas was in room 929 and was holding a press conference in fifteen minutes.

"Here in the hotel? It's dangerous."

"Where else would he find journalists?" the barman replied. He was known to be a messenger and "cutout" for the rebels.

I swallowed my glassful, paid up, and headed for the elevators.

On the ninth floor the Guardsman on duty asked to see my credentials. I passed them to him, and he smirked, and let me go down the corridor toward room 929.

Prudhomme was standing on the balcony fire escape peering down into the darkness of the city.

"He won't have anything to say," he told me, "and we shall be the only two in attendance. If we ask questions, we'll be honored with answers."

We finished our cigarettes and knocked on the door of room 929.

A woman opened it for us. She wore a pretty flowered housecoat and had curlers in her hair.

"You are here to talk Dale Carnegie?" she announced, loudly.

Prudhomme said that was surely the case.

She let us pass inside and slammed the door and slipped the chain in place.

A toilet flushed.

The bathroom door opened, and out stepped the leader of the proletarian movement, buttoning his fly. He peered at us through thick glasses and asked us to take seats. He sat on the bed. He was barefooted and so nearsighted it looked as though he could barely see his own feet.

"I am here to tell you," he said, "that we will launch another offensive in the sector around Chinendega tomorrow at dusk. Any questions?"

We had none.

He said, "We have maneuvered our movement so that it is in the forefront of the Revolution . . ."

I asked, "Can you be more specific?"

He gave Prudhomme a pained look and lowered his head. "I don't even have to tell you anything," he said.

The woman jiggled the chain. We were being asked to leave.

In the corridor Prudhomme asked how do you feel about stopping in Chinendega on the way back from Estelí?

"If we live so long," I said.

He offered to buy me a drink in the bar.

"I'll sit with you," I said. We went downstairs and the barman brought us two Victory beers and two *copas* of the brown rum.

"Are you worried about tomorrow?" Prudhomme asked.

"I'm worried every time I go outside the hotel," I said.

"Don't drink too much," he told me, swallowing a lot of beer.

I told him I would meet him in the lobby at four thirty in the morning. I'd tipped a bellman to prepare us a thermos of coffee.

In my room I undressed and turned down the air conditioner. I tried to read. I watched a football game on TV from Arizona.

Suddenly there was bang–bang all about the hotel and I rolled off the bed onto the floor. I could feel the building tremble, hear thuds and splintering glass.

A man called out in pain.

The lights went off.

I slept.

I woke at four and was in the lobby by four thirty. Two men were sweeping broken glass. The bellman told me the soldiers thought they had trapped an important "upstart" but he had gotten away when the generator failed.

Prudhomme came down the stairs. "It appears we don't have to go to the war, it comes to us," he said.

"Exactly," said the bellman.

He had coffee for us and a bag of sweet rolls. "There are soldiers all around the building," he explained. "Have your credentials ready when you enter the car park."

We drove north out of the city just as dawn was drenching the rich green hills with pink and orange sunlight. Most of the streets were empty. We passed through checkpoints of dozing militia and they glanced at our papers and at the strips of white bedsheet swirling from the antenna and passed us on.

Somewhere near the university a few old women stood head to head, as though conferring. As we came closer, we saw they were standing over a body.

Prudhomme stopped the car. There were streamers of blood on the cobblestones leading toward where the women stood.

"Have you got a camera?" one asked. "You should take *fotos.*"

"We carry nothing but pencils and notebooks," Prudhomme said. He asked what had happened.

The women explained the boy had been running from a patrol when he fell down from loss of blood and "died just as you see him."

They stepped aside so we could get a good look.

A pale youth lay on his side, his face staring off toward the gate of a nearby mansion. He was very slim and wore fancy Yankee cowboy boots.

I asked did anybody know who he was.

The women all shrugged at once.

Prudhomme said, "He's a martyr of course."

"*Seguro,*" one woman replied.

We started for our car again.

"Do we have to go to Estelí again today?" I asked when we were alone.

"Nobody says we do," Prudhomme replied.

He turned over the engine.

"We can stay beyond the *entrada* and watch from a rise," he added. "We don't need corpses in bulk."

"Let's go anyway," I said. "Let's just be careful."

"We won't do anything we shouldn't do," he said.

I said, "Maybe we won't go inside."

"Maybe . . ."

We lurched forward. By the time we got to Estelí the shooting had begun.

Prudhomme parked the car in an Esso station. We each took a strip of bedsheet. At the first Guardia checkpoint they told us we could only go as far as the fire station as the rest of the city was now a free shooting zone.

We made it to the bishop's residence and had fried potatoes and cold lemonade for lunch while they brought in casualties. By three in the afternoon we were heading back in the car again to be somewhere safe before curfew.

"What did you learn that you did not know before coming?" I asked.

Prudhomme said, "I'll be coming again tomorrow — that's all I learned."

We headed out along the main north-south highway toward the house of a "friend" in Chinendega. ●

CLANDESTINES (1981)

The lamp was crooked on the dark wood table; it tilted against the wall, a fancy Victorian china lamp with a bustle-shaped shade. Dust noodles dangled from the finial, as the servant problem was becoming severe. The light, like all other lights, was dim; electricity was sometimes in short supply. The lamp bulb trembled with a faint glow. One had the sense that it had been pushed to a teeter against the wall in this otherwise-proper-and-stuffy parlor a very long time ago.

Wanda Garza was neither old nor faded; she presided over the room with an air of frayed antiquated elegance. She sat very properly, with the dignity of a handsome forty-year-old, encased by a velvet Biedermeier settee. Her dark skirt was drawn across her knees. She was blonde, tanned, still rather pretty, her oval face seeming almost placid, almost serene, as she sat up with one elbow alongside the crooked lamp as though she were its guardian.

Her guest was tall and dark and awkward with his hands and feet. He spoke with a confiding air as he leaned forward from the hassock across the way at knee level. She called him Rik, though his name was Carl, and he seemed to do most of the talking, with an earnestness such as only younger men can display in argument.

"It just won't do to say it's not all their fault, Wanda. They wanted things this way." American, he spoke with the flat, accurate unmelodic colloquialism of the Midwest. "You know for yourself," he went on.

"But darling, what do I really know?" She addressed him in English. "I know they are all a bunch of children, whether Sandino's or not, and when children make mistakes it's different, I think. Such mistakes can always be corrected."

"Mistakes? I think they're doing just what they want to do," her guest insisted.

"You're harsh. They are children," she said. "These are just errors."

The hushed sudden spin of an overhead cooler fan made their voices sound extraordinarily detached, disembodied from the room itself, into which a servant in a white jacket entered with a glass pitcher of pink rum punch and two glasses.

"Please help yourself, Rik," Wanda said.

"In a little while." He was putting her off. "I really can't see why you're being so stubborn."

"Because I am Nicaraguan." Her teeth were very white when she smiled at him. "Now please may we talk about something else? Tell me about New York. How's Norman Mailer . . . and Elizabeth Taylor?"

"She doesn't live in New York," he reminded her.

"*Pues?*" She shrugged at him and laughed.

He decided he would risk reproaches and fix the lamp leaning against the wall. As he got up to come to her he said, in advance, "Excuse me."

Anticipating him, she leaned over and straightened the thing at its base, dislodging some dust.

"There, you see," she said. "It's harmless now. But it wasn't a while ago. During the Struggle I had that arranged with a charge inside to maim Ernesto, or even worse. He was always such a finicky person. Enough plastic to blow up the whole house. I didn't care. One more dead patriarchal fascist. I actually hated my husband. It turned out such measures proved unnecessary. When the situation got very bad here he went to Miami and divorced me."

He listened, as though from Wanda he expected unusual behaviors, but not viciousness. "Just to get Ernesto you would have booby-trapped the whole mansion?" he asked.

"If you supported the tyrant," she said, "I would do it to
you—and you know how very fond I am of you; I really
hated Ernesto. He was murdering people I loved. So why
should I have qualms? I always keep the lamp this way to
remember how it was then. It's strange . . . we learn certain
things like this, like this lamp, and we can never use them
again. Why should we?"

She shrugged, got up, straightened her skirts, came
closer, leaning over Carl, and then suddenly fell down
beside him. "I wish you could be more affectionate. You've
become so scolding about politics."

He seemed to shrug back at her. "I just can't believe you
don't see who these people are."

"And you do." She shrugged again and got up and stood
before the settee again. In the middle of the room, with her
hands outstretched, she seemed to implore some unseen
audience.

She made a face. "He won't fuck me anymore because he
doesn't like my friends?"

Carl wondered if the room was bugged.

He asked, "What's the matter now, Wanda?"

"Why not?" she demanded. "Why in God's name not?"

"How can I be with somebody who befriends gangsters?" he replied. "Thugs . . ."

She sat down again, dejected, an envelope flap without
any stickum.

"Why are you being so dramatic?" he asked.

"I want to be warm with you," she said. "Are you hungry? Do you want to cuddle?" She seemed to be treating
herself and Carl like two needy children. "Do you want to
make love together?"

Getting up, he told her, "I just think I'll go to my room
a little while."

"You really are a mule," she said then. "Go to hell."

She went up the stairs before he could, leaving him
alone in the cool dark room. Carl picked up a copy of one

of the Party papers and read about the latest currency restrictions.

When Wanda returned a few minutes later she wore a flowery orange and pink silk wrap, and had let her hair down. Her smile suggested she was prepared to be entirely forgiving, if he would only give her a chance. "What is it?" she demanded softly. "You've suddenly taken a dislike to women?"

"I'd just like to know where I am with you politically, among other things," he explained. "I don't want you getting hurt. And the way you keep shifting back and forth with me every time I see you I figure you're up for trouble . . . for yourself . . . for me . . . the whole shooting match."

"We appreciate your concern," she said. Then she addressed her unseen audience again: "Poor Carl. He's always been such a dear. He has this woman prepared to commit treason to her country every time she sees him and he still doesn't know where he is. Shall I show you?" She turned his way. "Shall I open up this wrap?"

"Not now!" He put up a hand before her eyes as though to ward her off.

"Very well." She went off behind the screen toward the kitchen. Above the roar of the fan, he shouted after her: "Don't be angry with me please. I still want you, I'm just a little troubled."

"It's not even your country," she called back, and appeared suddenly once more from behind the screen. "What troubles you? Why have you the right to be so arrogant?"

He started to say the situation was dangerous, but he dropped it. Carl really had no answer for her. He was only in Managua for a week or ten days this time, and she was probably right in saying it really wasn't his country, his problem. He had a valid U.S. passport, dollars in his pocket. He cared for this woman, but he could never babysit her. He'd said so many times to himself.

So why was he giving Wanda a bad time about that little gang of opportunists who were running things?

Carl seemed to feel her intimacy with them was ruining his intimacy with her.

They'd been together two days and it hadn't been the way it was in 1979 and 1980. More like he was going through the motions with a rather expert whore.

Wanda also denied he had rivals in the romantic sense of the word. She just tried to keep herself from getting lonely.

He felt contrite for his interrogations and insinuations.

"I'm really sorry for being such a bore," he told her. "I'll try to behave a little better."

She came out from behind the screen and walked toward him.

She came so close their bodies touched, and then their arms went about each other. They drew closer, hugging close. Wanda kissed Carl behind his ear. "You're such an attractive man," she said.

"The pleasure is all mine, señora."

"Well," she pouted, "*pues* . . . you could try to make it mine too."

She backed away and, in taking him by the hand, seemed to be leading him into the warm sea beyond her boudoir door.

He let her draw him along, though as he came abreast of the lamp, he noticed it was tilting again.

Just as before . . . as when she had told him about Ernesto.

Carl leaned toward Wanda to show her what was on his mind.

"Is this some king of a joke?" he demanded. "Your lamp. It's happening again."

"What do you mean? That?" She seemed truly incredulous. "Make love to me darling and I promise it won't happen to us."

Carl was spinning. "I'll fix it," he said.

"Don't!" She reached out for his hand.

"I can't stand it," he declared.

"Please," she said, "it won't bother us. You'll see. Don't."

"It will only take a second . . ."

"Don't," she pleaded. "Don't."

She succeeded in steering him up the staircase toward her bedroom.

Afterwards they lay together naked and sweaty, and the air was close, the cooler urging louder and louder vibrations on their ears.

She said, "You are very dear to me, Carl. Do you care for me too?"

"You know I do," he said.

She said, "If you want me to leave Nicaragua I will."

"That's nice." He turned over on his back. "Did you put a bomb in the lamp?"

"I love you, Carl," she repeated.

"What about the bomb?" he demanded. "Is it still down there?"

"It always has been," she said with another shrug, softly. "I never removed it. You get used to things and forget other people find them frightening. I let the thing be. I suppose I thought things haven't really changed that much . . . for any of us."

"Any of us?" He could feel his anger turning physical. He really wanted to hurt her. "You would blow me up?"

"Only if the sex was not too much, *cabrone*," she swore at him. "But you know better. So what are you so worried about?"

Carl continued to respond to her, to kiss and caress with methodical coldness. But when she went into the kitchen to prepare a snack, he dressed rapidly and ran down the stairs and out the front door.

In his hotel room he called the concierge and asked him to book a flight back to Miami at whatever cost.

"I am sorry you are leaving Nicaragua," the man said. "We'll all miss you."

"Not all of you," Carl said. "I wasn't that good a tipper and I always paid for everything with *cordobas*."

"You shouldn't be so cynical," the concierge said. "Life will improve. It has to."

"For your sake I hope so," he said.

The man said, "Just a minute," and then he told Carl he had a phone call.

"Say I've already checked out," he insisted. "I'm not here anymore."

He hung up.

Then he wrote to Wanda: "I don't doubt your desire for love, one way or the other. I wish I were somebody you cared about more. That probably couldn't be helped. Please don't try to hurt anybody unless it's in self-defense." ●

LITTLE SHARKS (1981)

At Doña Lara's Restaurant Prudhomme ordered so-called "little sharks" for us from Tipitapa. They came garnished with olives where there had once been eyes, and they were really quite delicious, as savory as the best of Veracruzian fish stews. Our waitress was old. She sucked on toothless gums as she complained about the price to us.

"For one of these fish," she said, "you could buy a bus ticket to San José and be done with Nicaragua Libre forever."

We ordered Cuba Libres made with raw white rum.

"The Bulgarians drink our nice old Ron Flor in Bulgaria. A temporary shortage, they say. Nowadays I serve only Germans."

"East or West?" Prudhomme asked.

"*Rubios,*" (blondes) she said, "though it may not even be so. They may have been Americans or even Russians."

The chef poured fat on his griddle and stood behind its sudden blaze dressed in whites. He had on Radio Havana blaring salsa, but he was a sellout if ever I met one. Just trying to please his American customers who all like Cuban music.

The waitress came back to tell us she had no more Coca but she could offer us sweet white wine from Mexico. It was syrupy like sauternes, or a cough syrup. Chilled, it slid right down the gullet and gave the fish an added savor. Presently our little sharks were flayed to the bones by our knives and forks, with only these rows of jagged sharp teeth menacing me.

There was only one other table with people taking a meal. A young couple from the country, dressed in elegant designer sport clothes, leaned their heads toward each other. The man had connections. He smoked Marlboro cigarettes and kept offering them to the chef and the old

35

crone who waited on us, and to us. The woman with him was as beautiful as he was dark and fat. She was fair with long jet black hair, a long pale neck. She also knew how to flirt and in just a few minutes I felt blushes invade my body.

Prudhomme said, "She likes you better than me, I'm afraid. Bad taste. The deprivations of war and Revolution."

"How would you know?" I teased. I knew, but I wanted to have my knowledge confirmed.

My shark grinned up at me. He seemed to propel himself off the plate and grab for my throat. Prudhomme hadn't noticed anything except the woman at the other table. "She's probably well born and probably a Sandinist with a small dollar account abroad for frequent shopping trips and so on."

"You don't say."

"Something like that. She could be a fascist I suppose." He winked. "I don't really know."

He winked again.

Stubbornly, after the fish Prudhomme ordered coffee and Ron Flors for ourselves, and also for the other couple. The waitress then produced four glasses lined at the bottom with a viscous amber fluid. She said the man, who was of Costa Rican nationality, was not awfully well pleased, but he knew how to be gracious. "See how he acknowledges your kindness with his own chin, señor?"

"Rudeness is always apropos," I said.

Prudhomme looked amused and then not amused. "It could be just my luck," he pointed out, "to be captured and tortured by my own side for one of my stupid acts of gallantry."

"Galantine is what jells around the ham," I said.

The fat gentleman came over to our table. He breathed like a saw going through wood. Were we Americans? How unusual. As a joke he opened his Guayabera and showed his designer T-shirt: white letters on a powder blue background.

COUNTER

INTELLIGENCE

"We don't have that brand in the States," I said.

"Of course not. You have CIA." He grinned.

Prudhomme said, "In France it's an alligator eating a beautiful woman."

"And what does it say?" asked the fat man.

"God and my gorey," Prudhomme said.

The fat man laughed. "I see."

Then he asked did we know of Alex Arguello, the great Nicaraguan prize fighter? Fatty said he was a *primo,* a cousin.

"But he's a Contra," Prudhomme pointed out.

"Not at all . . . hardly," the fat man said. "Alexei is maybe in a bit of a pout, like Pastora. They pout because their feelings are hurt. No real treason there. They'll get over it."

"That's not what I read in *Barricada,*" I said.

"We have to make it sound worse," the fat man said, "for the sake of the People."

He asked us to join him at his table for the second round of drinks.

I saw his lady sitting alone, as placid as a dahlia, and feeling my limbs start to tremble, was unable to refuse. When we got up from our table the woman rose from her table to greet us. We were introduced. Her name was Marisol and she was from the old Somocista middle class, though now she implied she was in the middle bureaucracy of the Ministry of Public Health, a nurse-supervisor. This was sort of their wedding anniversary. Her husband's name was Albert, but she called him Pacho. We were to help them celebrate.

"Calvin Klein," I said, and her husband said, "Come to think of it," but didn't finish.

Seated, I asked Marisol to her face what her husband did with the government. "Very little," she explained on his behalf.

She bade us make ourselves comfortable.

Their name was Arguello y Teiffel. They had cattle and gold and rice, but were good Sandinists. They declared they still had many things to protect.

"What do you think, as an American, of our new government?" she asked me.

"It beats the old I guess." I shrugged, at her, at all of us.

"My friend is not a philosopher," Prudhomme put in.

"And I think you look like an egg," I told this beautiful woman because I was suddenly very drunk.

Her husband was standing tall for a little fat man as though to call on his seconds. You could hear the wood yielding to his sawing. My insult was unintended; I quickly rewrote it.

"Such a perfect and elegant ovality of the ellipse," I pointed out. "Egglike is probably more like it."

The air seemed so bitter to taste. The man waved away the bad mood between us and produced his pack of cigarettes. "Care for a Marlboro?"

Then Prudhomme offered up some of his own portly and aromatic Celtiques.

Everybody thought they'd like to try. Taking fire, Fatso coughed. Abruptly, he offered us his wife. "As a Revolutionary courtesy," he said. "In solidarity. Really we're not even married."

"Then you are her pimp?"

"We are *compañeros;* we just called it an anniversary."

"He's her Revolutionary procurer," Prudhomme muttered, under his breath. "His real name's Camille Desmoulins."

"If you like." The fellow answered in French. "But I think you will find Marisol a wonderful woman. Men call her Yoya." She smiled at us.

Fatso informed us she had slept with Comandante Bayardo Arce and with old Chamorro's youngest daughter. She was a damn good friend of Humberto Ortega, brother of the Chief of State; and she had a child by Jaime Wheelock, who was probably gay.

"If she likes a gringo now," he went on, "it is because you are both friends of Nicaragua and because she don't speak too much English so I am always here to do it for her."

The woman remained placid, smiling down at her little amber glass of Ron Flor.

I asked where would we go? Where would I take her?

"Here on the restaurant table, *tout a coup,*" Prudhomme said.

"Of course not," Fatso replied. "We go to your hotel and I wait in the bar in the lobby."

"But I take too long."

"Then you buy me a room on account of the curfew," Fatso said.

"And what do I do?" Prudhomme wasn't kidding. "Where do I stay for the duration of this obscene act?"

"You will send dispatches back to *La Prensa,* which I, as counter-intelligence, will intercept." The man laughed harshly. The woman also put her hand up to her face and whispered something at her companion in Spanish.

He smiled at us weakly. "She says her blood is coming. She hopes you don't care."

"Certainly not," Prudhomme said. "We are both married men."

"*Bueno,*" said the pimp. "So now we must go tittle-tattle."

There was the bill to be paid and my sudden odd lack of interest, the grease of the fat man's smile. Something else needed to be said. What?

Prudhomme fingered his billfold for *cordobas,* the wilted browns and greens and oranges of exchange.

The woman reached over and plucked a five hundred *cordoba* note from his hands and smiling, as though for a camera, made it disappear somewhere into her clothing.

Prudhomme said, "I shan't even have her tonight but already she has me. *Mira.*"

"That's an old Nicaraguan expression you know." The fat man smirked. "The woman takes the man bakes. You have *picas*? Bites? On your legs? They say that when they mean randy."

Prudhomme pointed at me. "He's your man."

Outside darkness magnified the shadow of the big new moon above us. A security patrol passed as though trimmed with silver fittings.

He drove a large white *Citroen* bathtub sedan, a killer whale of a car with blue plush upholstery. When he unlocked the front door and sat down behind the wheel, I thought I heard him remark in English, "My aneurysm hurts me."

"So don't have sex," I said. "Take a valium."

I was in front. Prudhomme and the woman were in the back and they were necking. The man drove as though fording a river of congealed grease.

I heard the woman's breathing race against the sawing of her driver friend.

"I thought she was mine," I told Prudhomme.

"I am by far the bigger celebrity," he said. "This woman is an absolute star fucker."

"Don't stop," she urged him then, in English. "Don't talk."

We headed for the Intercontinental but suddenly veered toward the airport and the El Camino Motel. Nobody would know us there.

"I stayed in El Camino once," Fatso said, "and the pool was empty."

"Then you definitely are not a pimp," I said.

"I am not even in business any longer; I am a Minister Deputy of Posts and Telegraphs."

"Safe job," Prudhomme said. He seemed flustered. He lit one of his Celtiques and the woman coughed.

When we hit the other car there was a loud ripping sound, like Velcro unfastening.

Nobody cried out for fear of the police. The jeep belonged to the Fuerza Aérea. It was dark blue, I think, lying on its side, whereas we had only dents.

The soldier lying under it bled a lot and caught his breath and moaned.

"Somebody call an ambulance," the fat man said.

The woman had lost a tooth. I felt dizzy, achey. Prudhomme asked me to try with him to raise the jeep off the man's legs. With our arms up at a forty-five degree angle to the chassis, he said, "When we're done we'll just leave . . . we two my friend. The ambulance comes to do the rest. He hasn't got a chance this fellow."

"How do you know?"

"I tell myself that," Prudhomme said, "because I don't want to sleep in the Zona Franca Jail."

We heaved one more time and others pulled the man free. The jeep tumbled backwards noisily as we danced away.

Prudhomme said, "Ready? Let's go. I know the way."

The woman cried and called the fat man names. She argued with the caterwauling sirens which nobody in our party had summoned. "Do you have something for a tourniquet?" the fat man asked, as he knelt beside the injured man. He shouted to us, "*Compañeros,* . . . friends."

We ran through the narrow streets of Managua. Cats eyes glowed. Sirens seemed to greet us when we emerged at every corner. Too late I remembered the curfew.

Prudhomme said, "Let's hope this fellow dies. Otherwise he'll be at the inquiry."

Back at out hotel Prudhomme suggested a nightcap. "It's good nothing really happened," he observed. "Or I would have fallen in love with her."

"With that whore?"

"She was not," he insisted. "She was a maenad of the Revolution . . .*una compañera,* . . . but she has seen better days."

"Do you mean physically?"

"No. She is still beautiful, though up close you see she has hardly any teeth."

I asked if he was planning to stay in Nicaragua much longer.

"Hardly likely," he insisted. "In fact if you are packed we should drive to Costa Rica tonight."

Driving South from Managua, we saw the laborers of the southern *barrios* pushing their way through the darkness toward the early morning markets where they worked. We passed the wrecked jeep and the big white pod of the *Citroen* surrounded by pickets of gaudy pink flares.

A young sentry guarded them at parade rest.

Prudhomme said, "If looking makes you feel guilty, then you shouldn't of course."

We sped into what was left of the night. ●

TWO OF RIK'S AFTER DINNER STORIES (1984)

1

The Minister of the Interior took a delegation of the press to visit the Indians where they were incarcerated in a jail on the outskirts of Managua. He brought along TV cameras and strobes. This would be a feed for the evening news. He had an important announcement to make. From where he stood, dramatically lit, upon the makeshift podium, Comandante Borge told the Indian prisoners assembled in the darkness below his feet that he was going to free them all and give them land away from the East Coast where they could farm and live in communities again. They could "sing their own songs, dance their own dances, pray to their God." All he asked was that they not make war against the government.

The cameras swayed and the strobes moved out among his audience, lighting the darkness of a perfectly placid oil painting. Nobody applauded their deliverances or seemed in the least bit animated. Borge looked perplexed. He glanced from aide to aide for explanations.

Finally a young Indian in the crowd raised his hand and explained to the *"muy estimado comandante"* that not a single person in his audience understood Spanish. Could he take the liberty of explaining it all to them in Miskito? "We think differently and have our own language," he pointed out.

"These people are so backward," a Nicaraguan journalist told me.

Borge was more gracious; he permitted the translation to go forth in a stream of words which sounded like liquid Bolivian flutes resounding across a high Andean plateau.

Later, at dinner, in the restaurant above Tiscapa volcano, the Minister said the Nicaraguans had often wronged the Indians and he hoped his program would make amends. We all sat together in a glow of Japanese lanterns. "The Indians would be given land," he said, "inland, for the lands the government had confiscated on the East Coast. They would only have to work it for themselves."

We sat in the roseate light and Borge was funny and rhetorical, a very small ogre full of apt dramatic gestures. His hand was soft and warm and pliant when he shook hands with everybody to say goodnight.

The next morning I read in the Financial Times that the government was hoping to grant a concession of many thousands of acres to the British Tobacco Company and had promised to supply the British capitalists with labor and tax incentives.

2

When Danilo Ortega was inaugurated as president, a lot of top Hollywood people showed up in Managua. They expected and received VIP treatment: reserved seats at the swearing in, interviews with leading officials, fine meals, perhaps some toot. A couple of high-ranking studio officials and their dates were even granted an audience with Fidel Castro, who was also visiting.

Castro is said to be a film lover, but, though he spoke to them in an informal way, he talked politics mostly, into the early hours of morning. One dream merchant, who came attired in a white dinner jacket and sneakers, according to Prudhomme, the sine qua non of schlock chic, apparently had a yen to do something white and powdery all night long because he interrupted Fidel, right in the middle of a long, thoughtful harangue about U.S. and Latin American relations, to say the hour was getting late and they had surely been over this ground many times already.

"When I am talking to you, don't interrupt," the Cuban leader replied sharply. He went on talking for another hour or more.

"It was just like a movie," said Prudhomme. "You know what I mean? Fidel is a great actor and he knew his audience. They were impressed. Nobody said another word until he was finished, and the next day they all left Nicaragua." ●

CAFÉ (1981)

At an outdoor table at the café near the big hotel sat the officer from the North, with an AK-47 next to him. He surveyed vast acres of rubble and bulldozed terrain which occupies so much of the old center of the city, as though on guard against an uprising of cadavers. Next to him, in chic civilian military-style *mufti,* a group of young snobs discussed the results of a beauty contest in San Juan Sur with considerable animation. Some were sons and brothers of important people in the government and seemed not in the least discomforted that their subject was considered inappropriate to current public mores in Nicaragua.

"I can assure you this was not girlfriends first," said a fair young man with long, almost female, black eyelashes. "That woman looked like she took in laundry."

A youth with heavily-lidded eyes intervened, "What do you know about women? I've been all over the world and I have to say"—he spoke with honeyed malice—"the body is everything."

"You are so vulgar," a third said.

"Nobody tells me that." The heavy-lidded youth raised a bottle of beer off the table as though to brain his companion.

"Boys, please." The officer rose to restrain him. Facing them all, he said, "It could be put better but he's quite right. I know from war—when the body dies what else is there?"

"A woman has beauty aside from her sex," said the youth with the bottle.

> Your red flower mouth
> and your green eyes
> fill with sun . . .

"Death to Somocism, bandit," jeered the officer. "We all know what Ernesto Cardinal says and what he does are different. It's make believe."

46

The waiters were all at militia drill so the niece of some-one, Gabriella, waited on them. She was very pretty and some men said stuck-up. Now she came with a rag to clean and clear, and the officer gently patted her on the rump, as though they were old acquaintances.

"Get your hand off my ass," said Gabriella. "There you have the Revolution to me in a nutshell."

She shook him off but his hand returned as soon as she stopped moving. "Your hand," she reminded him.

"Tell me my beauty," he said, "if you treasure more your body or your mind."

"*Cabrone,* my mind can't kick you in the eggs if you mis-behave, and it can't wait on tables and collect tips."

He took his hand away from her. "That's well put. Your mind can't even lie in its throes with that young student over there." He was pointing to the boy with the long eye-lashes who'd started the whole discussion by mentioning the beauty prize was unmerited.

Seeing the young fellow blush, the officer knew he'd touched on a truth about Gabriella and the student, and he laughed, taking pleasure in the fact that his hand was once more on her rump and she was saying nothing to protest.

He grew bolder: "Tell me, angel, who do you think is more beautiful—María Merced, our new queen of pulchri-tude, or you as you stand here now with my hand on your rump?"

She was angry. "Give me two dogs mating in the street any day in the week," she sneered, and she pulled away from him and went back into the kitchen.

"Don't feel badly," one of the youths said. "The Chief of State has eight or nine children, so he must have done it at least that many times."

A peddler started down the block toward them:

Red bananas
Roast bananas
Yucca . . .

The boys were making jokes among themselves.

The officer sat by himself, withdrawn from his environment, and presently required a check.

Gabriella swept the front steps as though dancing for everybody on the terrace.

"If you ask me," said the *patrón* behind his cash drawer, "this Revolution has made us more considerate of each other but also more stupid." ●

SUCKING CHEST WOUNDS (1978)

In twilight the man in the back of the van reclined heavily upon his hand and forearm; his face was greenish, and he seemed to be having trouble breathing. We could hear raspy noises.

Prudhomme had first-aid compresses doused with medication, and he told the man to lie back and "hold this" against his chest. "You have a sucking chest wound," he told the man. "And if this driver gets you to Managua in time you will be okay." He turned to me and added, in a whisper, "If not he will surely choke on his own blood."

The man rasped thanks loudly and and fell backward and reached for the surgical dressing. Prudhomme climbed into the van and knelt and pressed it to the man's chest. He backed out in a hurry and seemed to fall backwards through the open doors of the van.

"Quickly," he called to the driver. "Hurry." The van lurched and kicked up dust. We stopped in the twilight. "Where shall we go now?" he asked. "Hotel," I said. We started walking toward the car, but at the turning in the road stood a National Guard jeep with two soldiers at port arms. They'd parked alongside our car.

"What are you doing out here?" asked a non com.

"We needed some air," Prudhomme said. "We're heading back now."

He pointed to all the white sheets fluttering from our car: *Reporteros . . . periodistas.*

"Pieces of shit," said the non com, as he was driven off. They went fifty paces down the road, spun wide, and made a U turn, heading straight toward us with .50 caliber pointed. Then they veered and headed northward toward La Paz Centro.

We were on a stretch of two-lane Highway connecting Managua and León. Prudhomme tried starting the car, but the engine wouldn't turn over. It was getting darker.

"We'll have company sooner or later," he said, "and ask for a boost."

After a little while, a big semi with Honduran plates drew alongside, blaring its horn. We heard it coming from some distance away. Prudhomme stuck his head out the window and explained to the dark bald man behind the wheel that we were stuck, battery trouble. He said he would come behind us and give us a push and we could freewheel down the next incline and turn over the motor.

The truck seemed to low and moan; it was filled with cattle being smuggled out of the country by Nica land-owners who knew the Regime was failing. They'd bank the profits in Honduras and book seats on the next TACA flight out.

When the truck came up behind us there was a clattering of hoofs. Cattle were tumbling willy nilly. The truck crept up on us slowly and then banged us forward. We started to roll. Again it banged us on. We rolled to the brim of the next hill, and then there was another bang and we started down fast, almost out of control.

"Hit the clutch in neutral," I shouted at Prudhomme. The engine caught and whined, full throttle, and then slowed and softened as we went into gear, then pulled to the side of the highway to let it rev.

The truck surged past, horns blaring. *"Gracias,"* shouted Prudhomme, but the semi was making too much noise, and his words probably weren't heard. We stayed by the side of the road purring in the darkness, afraid to turn on lights, for another half hour or so, for fear the battery would die on us again.

It was very dark and a little chilly. Way beyond curfew by the time we came to the squatter settlement of Open Tres on the outskirts of Managua. The Guardia had blocked the road; a gunfight was taking place among the shanties. We got out and walked to the Command Post.

Prudhomme immediately recognized Major Simpson of the Military Police and took me over to greet him.

The major was covered by a big green rubber pancho, as though expecting rain, and he seemed to be in a very heavy sweat.

"It's these bullet-proof vests," he explained. "You can't breath with one on, so you sweat a lot. I doubt if it helps finally."

"Not so long as your head sticks up," I said.

"Anyway it protects my eggs," Simpson said, peering down in the general direction of his aproned genitals.

A bullet whacked the side of his CP panel truck. Glass splintered.

Prudhomme said, "You can't make a revolution without cracking Simpson's eggs."

"It don't matter nowadays," the Major replied, glumly. "All the women only want the Sandinista."

"Push coming to shove," I said.

"*Maricones,*" Simpson said. "Sissies." Prudhomme said, "Those sissies have more than just .22s inside there."

"Of course, they have a *cinquenta,* .50 caliber," Simpson said, "stolen off a motorpark jeep and an old Browning. When morning comes I'll call for an air strike."

"*Mucha gente,*" I cautioned, meaning civilians.

"It's war," Simpson replied.

Prudhomme asked if he would let us through to Managua as it was way past curfew.

"You wait fifteen minutes I'll give you a safe conduct," he said.

He went inside the truck and got on the phone.

Then they brought in two Guard casualties, a headless corpse and a young dark boy with a sucking chest wound just like that of the boy in the van, the same green pallor and raspy breathing.

Prudhomme had one more dressing in his kit so he showed a sullen corporal how to apply it to the boy's chest.

"What if I take a bullet now?" he asked me.

The major's aid found us and told us we could move on now, the way was cleared. We ran to our car and started driving.

Half a mile beyond "Open Tres" the car bumped and thumped and limped to one side, a tire with a sucking hole the size of a silver *duro,* we discovered when we got out and shined a light on it; probably a bullet hit. We had a spare and made quick work jacking up the car and turning the lug wrench. In another half hour, we were entering Managua, but we'd forgotten to get that safe conduct from the major and it was after one in the morning. Prudhomme thought we might park on the street and walk to the hotel to avoid the Guardia patrols.

We started down an alleyway of wrecked and over-grown building sites, part of the destruction that still existed from the earthquake of '73. There was no moon but the stars seemed to curdle overhead in large thick clots.

If we kept going we would reach the parking lot of the hotel, but we would have to skirt the wall of the infantry training base. I suggested we veer a little to the right across an open field.

The great fake Mayan pyramid of the hotel was brightly lit, and we heard the sounds of Muzak wafting off one of its numerous patios, the theme from the movie *Exodus,* as I recall.

Prudhomme and I were hip deep in garbage and trash. "Let's just hope there are no snakes," he announced.

I thought the corpse we almost stumbled over was a boulder; it lay on its belly with its back bunched high, and it was covered with a dark military tarp. The smell of rot was unmistakable. I thought it must be a soldier, or a very big dog, but I didn't wish to look, and Prudhomme said, "Let's keep walking. We can't help the poor sod."

We crossed a military motor park without sentries, and then the hotel parking lot, and as we stepped out into the lighted area in front of the hotel, a battered taxi lurched forward and the driver, in serviceable English, said, "Good evening, sirs, it's later than you think. Would you gentlemen care to meet some ladies?"

There were two mousy little whores in the back of the cab and they both were smiling, with lipstick on their teeth.

Prudhomme explained we were both much too tired after a hard day.

"Another time perhaps," the driver said.

"Maybe," I said.

"Surely," he asked. "When?"

"If we're ever interested, we'll look for you," I said. "What do you call yourself?"

"Ask for *Matrimonio*," he said, which can mean a sexual position as well as marriage. "Everybody knows *Matrimonio*. I am your man."

We started up the hotel steps.

Prudhomme asked, "Do you want a drink?"

"Maybe," I said. "In my room."

"You are feeling unfriendly?"

"Just a little tired," I said.

"Goodnight," he said, and headed toward the bar.

The Guard had been going through my things. Clothes lay on the floor of my closet and my suitcase was spilled across the rug.

Everything was a confusing mess, but it would have to wait until morning for me to straighten things out.

I took off my shoes and lay down on the bed fully clothed to smoke a cigarette. Closed my eyes, put the cigarette in my mouth, but waited to light up, and the next thing I knew it was morning and there were shreds of tobacco all over the sheets and a taste in my mouth of ashes and burnt bones. ●

IN TEGUCIGALPA (1987)

A slim man with military shoulders stood among the gaming tables at the hotel casino. He wore a gray civilian suit of raw silk and a red silk shirt, open at the collar. Just as the roulette wheel started to spin, he caught the croupier's attention and passed him a brand new thousand-dollar bill, and told him he wanted it all on red. He seemed to be a little wobbly on his feet, his eyes giving back little pinpoints of light.

"Not such a gamble," he pointed out. "I put my money on red because communism will prevail in Honduras."

The wheel spun and spun and softly clicked into place in front of a low black number.

"Oh shit," he said, and walked silently away from the tables, with his hands in his pockets, toward two uniformed aides who waited for him on the other side of the gaming room entrance.

"I just got no more luck," I heard him say.

A young noncom told his colonel if he bought chips he would lose his money more slowly.

"You got time for that?" the man stopped himself to shout. "I don't got so much time anymore."

He walked into the lounge bar and sat down upon a divan while his escort waited at the entrance.

The colonel ordered a Scotch and signed his name to a chit. He gave the barman a dollar tip.

"I just hate losing," he said, loudly so I could overhear.

"Be more careful, brother," the barman said.

"What you say?"

The barman shrugged and wiped his bar.

A soldier approached me where I stood, next to a big potted plant, and asked what I was looking at.

"In my whole life," I said, "I never until now saw a thousand-dollar bill."

"Money is all you Yankees think about," he said.

He asked me if I would move on.

I asked what was this officer's name and where was he posted.

"He's retired now, in business."

"Any particular sort?"

"He loses money all the time," the soldier said. "It's a big bad business for him. Lousy."

"That's too bad. What sort of business?"

"Eggs," the soldier said. "He sells eggs."

"For a thousand dollars?"

"You don't see too good," he said. "Maybe it was only a hundred, but these are great big eggs."

"Any particular type?"

"Hard boiled," he said, "with tomatoes."

So that was that. The colonel finished his drink and was coming toward us. "You want an egg?" he asked me. "Brother, that will cost you a lot."

"Too much," I said.

"It's such a big egg," he told me. "A big shell."

He started back toward the casino and when he entered he produced another like-new bill—a hundred.

"Remember to buy chips this time," his noncom said.

The colonel himself placed the bill on the green felt as everybody else edged backwards.

The wheel spun, clicked on red, and settled into a black slot.

"Fucking thieves," he said. "I work hard for my money."

He produced a gun.

Just then one of the men playing the slots grabbed at him from behind in a full nelson and told him to please put his weapon down on the table right away.

"Everybody takes advantage," the colonel said. "That's communism."

He walked out of the room and through the lobby, escorted by two soldiers and the man from the casino, who handed him back his weapon just as soon as they were outside. ●

SOME ELVES FOR THE SHOEMAKER (1984)

Carlo Galan first buried his ancient Luisita in Monimbo soil beneath the cemetery wall during the fighting of Little Summer, 1978. He'd been given the weapon out of gratitude in 1934 by one of Sandino's *guerrilleros* whom Carlos hid and fed while the man was fleeing to Costa Rica. The machine gun was a large, cumbersome thing with a horizontally mounted cartridge drum, the sort of gun one found mounted in the back seat of squad cars and biplanes before World War II. For years Carlo kept his Luisita packed in Cosmoline grease and wrapped in an old blanket on a top shelf of his workshop among lasts and odd bits of steel, wood, and leather.

From the beginning of the Revolution Carlo said to himself his gun might be needed someday, though not now. There were others around to fight. When the open street ambushes started, he knew the rebels would win, though it wouldn't be easy, and victory would not end repression. He came to regard the Luisita as his insurance. Buried in the earth somewhere, next to the cemetery wall, it could later be unearthed and used to liberate himself and others, not pitted up or wasted by young kids with crazy nerves and funny masks.

Carlo was not really opposed to the Revolution. He regarded change as inevitable, and he hoped it wouldn't stop with old Somoza. He and his friends had certainly not received benefits from the change in power yet. If it had happened for others, it was still to come for him, just as some Jews regard Christ as a premonition, not an achievement. Out of love and fear, Carlo remained a skeptic.

Stowed six feet underground in a crypt, the Luisita was protected against rust. Like a mourner, he went about his shoemaking above ground throughout the fighting, and the victory, and the consolidation of Sandinist power. When the loudspeaker trucks toured the *barrio* offering amnesty now to those who turned in their weapons, Carlo devised a little doggerel to remind him of who he really was and what he possessed:

My Luisita
is a pretty woman.
If you squeeze her
she goes crazy.
So many little bullets
could make cheese from a stone wall.
She's sleeping now
but when she wakes
she'll have a tantrum
in her bed, and then
whoever bothers us is dead.

Carlo was sort of the unofficial local *cacique,* but he never recited his poem to the people of the *barrio.* He always spoke sparingly and had very little advice to give others. How it got around to Sandinist police that he had a Lewis gun buried nearby with lots of ammo could only be attributable to old neighbors. Such a rumor had circulated shortly after his Sandinist guest departed for Costa Rica. It never went away. The new rulers of Nicaragua worried as much about weapons that remained unauthorized and had not yet been turned in, despite two amnesties, as did the brutes of old Somoza's National Guard. They let it be known through the neighbors that the wrong people might find Carlo's stash of weapons and commit terrorism.

Carlo replied, "This is the gun of Sandino. The *gringos* preferred the Browning."

And he told no one where his Luisita was buried.

For a few weeks handbills were issued to all the *barrio* reminding residents that weapons of larger caliber than the

.22 hunting rifle were considered contraband, and there was to be no storage of contact bombs or other high explosives. Residents were encouraged to consider active voluntary service in the militias. But Carlo, who lived a few doors away from the Museum of the Revolution, which had been designated a collection point, refused to respond.

The local Party officials still wished to be sensitive, if they could, to the feelings of residents of Monimbo, "the birthplace of the Revolution." They posted a Nahautl-speaking spy inside the *barrio,* and every market day the sound truck appeared and broadcast the official communiqué about unauthorized weapons and the amnesty for those who still had them.

"Monimbo is Nicaragua," Carlo told his girlfriend, Juana. "Your shoes pinch so they say they will remove your toes."

"Not so loud," she told him in Indian.

He was a respected figure in Monimbo, but some people began to wonder if his recalcitrance would bring them trouble.

Carlo lived alone. His ten-year-old son lived two doors away with his mama, and he was always visiting his father to learn about making shoes and about the *corneta* which the shoemaker played with great flair.

Marianno was a fine young lad with colossal eyes like black olives and he was devoted to his father, in part, because of the legend of the Luisita.

Coming back from school one day, Marianno noticed some men digging near the tomb of German Falli Abreto, a martyr of the Revolution. They also had a thing like a vacuum cleaner which he thought was detecting metal. Marianno ran to his father's house to warn him of what was going on.

The shoemaker sat at his last wearing white cotton gloves as he fashioned shiny patent leather pumps for a wealthy male customer in Managua.

"This style of leather always spots," he explained to his son.

The boy told him what he'd just seen.

"They won't find anything," Carlo said. "Let them dig up old Somoza and all they'll have is bones, not my Luisita."

"Why not?" asked the boy.

Carlo did not wish to go into details. "It was entombed," he pointed out, "and soon it will rise. World without end, amen."

Puzzled, perplexed, the boy hung around a little while and then went home to help his mother build a fire.

Left to himself, Carlo was angry. He was no terrorist. Why wouldn't they leave him alone about the gun? He decided to dig the thing up that evening and find a better hiding place.

Carlo remembered the foreign journalists in Monimbo during the fighting years. He'd sheltered some and had his picture taken as a symbol of "Monimbo's defiance." Once he told a young woman about the Luisita. "It will take more than your old gun to liberate Monimbo, old man, " she reminded him.

"Who could argue with you?"

She asked if he would take a picture holding it, but Carlo refused. "Some things should be left in reserve," he pointed out.

When darkness came the woman left and did not return again. He later learned she was famous.

"I don't trust people who take your picture and then run away," Carlo told Juana.

"Maybe you have reasons," Juana replied. "And she had reasons, too."

It was so dark when Carlo went out later that he didn't bother to wear clothing. He closed the shutters about his small house and grabbed a shovel and started walking in the hot night air in his underpants toward the cemetery wall.

A militia sentry was stationed next to the ruins of the old Guardia *cuartel* which Carlo helped others burn to the ground with five soldiers inside in the late summer of 1978.

He recognized the youth as the son of his old friend, Segunda. Staying close to the wall of the chapel, he made his way around to the privy on the other side.

The night was full and black; there were no stars. He got down on his hands and knees and pried away some loose boulders and then began to pick at the loamy black earth with the end of his shovel.

A voice called out, "Who is there?" Carlo kept still.

He knew his greasy old gun could not defend him against a Kalishnikov.

He regretted running out naked as he had. He was so much more vulnerable, though either way he would surely bleed. They have all the weapons.

"I see your ass," the militia youth said. "Identify yourself."

"I am just nobody anymore," Carlo said. "Just an ass, boy."

"I could shoot," the boy said. "Who are you?"

"The worm," he said. "He's working, please, so don't disturb."

He pulled away some more earth and stones and felt the gun like a skeleton, bestowed beneath his hands.

He would let the thing be a while longer, and had covered it over with his hand when he felt the point of a rifle digging into his ribs.

"Maldito suerte," Carlo cursed.

From the look on little Segunda's face he didn't recognize his father's old friend.

Carlo said, "I must have eaten a *fer de lance* for my dinner. Such cramps I had . . .

"Identify yourself," the boy said.

"I am Carlo Galan," he said, rising, but in so doing he probably frightened the youth, who fired into his side point blank, killing him instantly.

The captain was summoned, and when the boy saw his victim really was Carlo Galan he was contrite.

Now that Carlo was dead, the government didn't search for the gun anymore, and it was never found. Eventually a new privy was put up right on the spot where Carlo had been digging.

There are rumors among the Indians of Monimbo that the earth on which they squat will someday liberate them.

Carlo Galan's son no longer lives in Monimbo.

In the dense fields outside town some boys fabricate little bombs and practice marksmanship with sticks and hunting rifles.

If you are afraid of death, they will tell you, you will almost surely die. ●

THE SECRET
ADMIRERS (1979)

"You see that man with the knobby red knees sitting by the pool?" Prudhomme said. "That's Graham Greene."

"The writer Graham Greene?" I asked.

"Exactly," he said. "He comes here to Nicaragua often and never leaves the pool, but he knows everything that's going on. He knows Torijo in Panama and all the big shots. You should go over and say hello."

I looked again: Greene seemed scrawny, frail, a little bent with age. I didn't have anything to say, didn't wish to say anything.

Prudhomme said, "He usually reads his *Financial Times* and then people drop by for a drink and a chat. Important people. Don't you want to talk to him?"

"No," I said. "Not at all. Do you?"

"I'm French," Prudhomme pointed out. He gave me a look of such entire incredulity that I felt I should apologize. "He's only one of the major writers of our time," Prudhomme said. "Decorated by many nation-states, and a Nobel also ran. Now you don't wish to say toodeloo?"

"That's goodbye," I said.

"Suit yourself." He shrugged me off and went over to where Greene was sitting and commenced a conversation. For just a moment they seemed very engrossed with each other and then Prudhomme pointed his body my way and motioned at me.

The great writer nodded his gaunt florid face, and I stared at my sneakers and fussed with my cigarettes.

After a while I felt Prudhomme was standing next to me again and I looked up.

He said, "Mr. Greene believes the U.S. could invade Nicaragua before the New Year."

"Or even after," I said.

"I suppose," Prudhomme allowed, smiling.

"What did you tell him about me?" I asked.

Prudhomme was twisting his mustache: "I said you were CIA."

"Aces."

"And he said he'd free-lanced for MI 6 in Mexico, among other places."

"Marvelous," I said. "And you are KGB?"

"Second Bureau," he averred.

"Well, I appreciate you putting in the good word for me," I said.

"Don't be sensitive, Richard."

"If I were CIA I'd be sensitive."

"You're much too sensitive," Prudhomme said.

"If I were CIA," I said.

"Everybody is in the States," he said. "What else would you be?"

"Maybe," I said, "I'm with the National Gay Task Force."

Prudhomme's laugh was like a dog's bark. "I'm kidding. You're kidding too. No?"

We glanced over at Greene. He sat there like a big iceberg melting, the great cold bulk of his past life remaining underwater.

Prudhomme pulled me toward the bar. I asked, "Did you really tell him I was CIA?"

"I told him you were shy." He barked again.

"Thanks a lot," I said.

"You are much too sensitive," Prudhomme said. "Mr. Greene isn't sensitive. He talks to Fidel and doesn't ever pretend he wasn't with MI 6. He's a man of the world."

He ordered two rum Cocas.

"You know, Richard," he said, "there are KGB people everywhere and they are just like everybody else, but these days they dress a little better."

"Like you?" I inquired.

He peered at me over the rim of his glass.

"I'm like you," Prudhomme said. "I'm shy."

"And I'm Saul Zabar the lox king," I said.

"The what?"

"Never mind."

"Are you really shy?" he demanded.

"Let's go talk to Graham Greene," I said.

"Not now. The writer expects important visitors."

"I'm glad," I said, "relieved."

"And I'm shy," he laughed. And ordered another drink. "Who else would you like not to meet?"

"Gabriél García Marquez?" I declared. "Cortazar?"

"Not available," said Prudhomme, "by reason of death in Cortazar's case, and Gabo is in Europe. What about Bianca Jagger?"

"I didn't meet her the last time I was here."

"No way I could improve on that," he told me. "Would you care to meet some minor Costa Rican communists?"

"Frankly," I said, "I'd prefer an anarcho syndicalist from Belize."

"They're all too shy. Have another drink."

"I think I'll introduce myself to Mr. Greene now," I said. I started away from the bar.

"You could tell him you are me," Prudhomme said.

"Why would I want to do that?"

"Because I told him I was someone else." He squirmed against his stool.

"What did Mr. Greene say?"

Prudhomme seemed delighted with himself. His smile shattered the glass in his hands when he brought it to his lips. He waited me out as though to gauge my patience with him.

"Tell me," I demanded.

"Ah, it's very obvious really. The distinguished British writer asked me, 'Aren't you CIA?' "

"Son of a bitch."

"Yes, that too," said Prudhomme, "so I told him no, I am simply shy."

"Did you say that?" I asked.

"No," he said, "I told him I was with the National Gay Task Force."

"Very funny, Victor."

"It's better than Saul Zabak," Prudhomme said. He peered at me coldly. "There are always secrets in the world. Don't you know that? There always will be."

Dismissing me with his eyes, he attended to a fresh drink. ●

MARITAL DIFFICULTIES (1984)

The Santos were having marital difficulties: she was pregnant by another man in the Ministry and wanted to be aborted. Solomon, on the other hand, was still as Catholic as Holy Week. Abortion was murder to him. "If you want this man," he told Rosey, "I will leave you. If you don't want the child, I will raise him for us in a separate house until the day you do. But you must not murder love."

Rosey was still young and very pretty. She loved Solomon because he was kind, but she was in love with this other man for selfish reasons. She felt a clock inside her whirring. Abortion was possible, but the State needed children. She did not like seeming "selfish."

She went to see a woman doctor in the Diriamba Clinic and then spoke with the Salesian priest, who was an old school friend and no enemy of the Revolution. Finally she agreed to have the child because "more than I need to leave, my husband needs me."

Staying with Solomon worked out at first: the other man only visited on rare occasions, if there was a militia encampment; and she came to prefer Solomon's attentions. The neighbors said, "While Solomon protects his home and family she gets in the family way." Pregnant again, Rosario couldn't be sure who the father was.

That all happened during the winter of the False Invasion, when most everybody broke their backs digging tank traps in their spare time and nobody had any energy left over for romantic adventures, except for certain bureaucrats. Rosey's lover came one night eight months later and was surprised to find Solomon answer the front door.

"Hello," he declared, "I must have the wrong address."

"You are looking for Mr. Horn?" Solomon asked wryly.

"No, no, nothing of the sort," the man said. "I'm sorry to have disturbed."

"Is there anything else you are sorry for?" Solomon demanded.

"Nothing of the sort," the man said. But he backed away and ran down the alley.

That evening in bed Solomon told Rosario that since they only had boys he would like to try for another child.

"I won't say no," she told him, seductively.

"And this time," he added, "I want it to be *my* child."

"As you like . . ."

They both started laughing and then they were holding each other, and through the night they laughed and held each other. As the neighbors say, that was the last anybody ever saw of Rosario's lover in the house of Solomon Santos. ●

THE ANVIL OF THE TIMES (1984)

In the middle of the night the Vega family often heard strange loud cacophonies, as though metal were being tortured or twisted. That was because they lived near a motor park where lorries battered by age and ill-use, as well as combat, were being readied to roll north toward the border and remove casualties from the struggle there to the nearby military hospital. The work went on night and day, and it was often said that the most creative geniuses of Nicaragua were all auto mechanics. One night, though, the urgency of what was being done to metal was piercing, exhausting. It sounded very much like sharp whining cries in the night. Some new sort of lathe, they told themselves, was on line, and they hardly slept all night long.

The next morning they walked about as though enmeshed in cobwebs. Right next door to the machine sheds a big lot looked hot and vacant. Patricio Vega felt so exhausted he did not go to work, but went off to the store to buy fresh milk for the children. While he was gone a party of Scandinavians arrived in an open jeep. They were from a certain international agency, intent on gauging living standards among the inhabitants of the Vega's *barrio*, and were accompanied by a PR person from Managua. Could they come inside the house to talk?

"Of course." Felicia Vega opened her door wide for her visitors. Her husband would be home soon. Wasn't he at work? She explained about last night and taking the day off and the government person frowned.

"How do you explain to these good people," the man asked, "how you own your own house, feed your family, are clothed as well as anybody who is not an office worker, and your husband only goes to work when he pleases?"

"It's because we have always been good Nicaraguans," she smiled at him, waxily.

Just then Patricio appeared in the doorway: *"Hola."*

He recognized the government man. "Aren't you the son of Andres Perra from Zelaya?" Patricio asked.

"That sort of thing doesn't matter here any more," young Perra said. Their Scandinavian visitors looked a little downcast, but when they heard the coffee boiling began to produce their soft pencils and questionnaires.

Young Perra told Patricio: "We're here to dispel some myths about life under the regime. I assume you will want to be cooperative."

"I'll be glad to tell the truth," Patricio said.

"He's a bit of a rascal," young Perra confided. "They all are. The children are our only hope."

"Probablemente," said a big Swede in Spanish.

Felicia Vega was noted throughout town for her custards, which were said to be as sweet and rich as two weeks in Miami, but when she offered to serve some to her guests along with their coffee, Patricio grew indignant. "Can't you tell what kind of men these are? They're snobs toward the likes of you and me!"

"I'm sure the Swedish gentlemen would love some custard," young Perra observed, "if it were hygienic."

"If it were not," Patricio said, "I would offer it to you. You could replace its scum with yours."

"You are a fool to talk like that," Felicia said.

"Listen to your wife," young Perra added.

"Forgive me," he replied, with mock earnestness.

Patricio was a small dark intense man, with big eyes and shiny black hair. He seemed a man of strength, but was really a kind of intellectual: by days he worked at the refinery and evenings he took courses in French literature and philosophy at UNAM.

Nobody approved of his ambitions; nobody understood them. He was determined to be a philosopher, and, though Marx was where he began, he was no longer a Marxist. He called himself "post-Christian man."

Whenever he had words with a person in government, Patricio withdrew into a deep cauldron of philosophic silence. He could truly say no more for fear of becoming violent. "Even if you shut up nowadays," he reminded friends, "they know you are their enemy."

So it was, much against his wishes that the wife of Patricio Vega went to her cold chest and removed the large bowl of milk custard, and suddenly the small room was redolent with the smells of nutmeg and cinnamon. The Swedes exclaimed even before they'd been served, "Marvelous!"

"Our Nicaraguan cuisine is not to be denied," said young Señor Perra.

"Indeed," said one aging Swede whose unruly blonde hair had long since turned as white as flax.

More chairs were brought to the table, and wooden spoons and Earthenware bowls. A young Swede found his questionnaire and commenced to ask, "Do you believe living conditions are better or worse now than before?"

"I'll answer that," Patricio said. "They are clearly better now. Before we had no PR men on our hands. Now they cannot help but be better."

"He's known to be a wit," Perra said.

"Shut up. You are in my house." He turned to the Swedes. "Ask my wife how she likes standing in line hour after hour for pig shit."

"Some people expect us to manufacture brasssières in the middle of a famine," young Perra mocked. He seemed a little flustered and immediately suggested that after the visitors finished their custards, they should all go to a more interesting and cooperative household.

"These good people mean no harm," said an elderly balding Swede. "They simply need to speak out."

"In the face of disaster," said young Perra, "that is not always our privilege. It's not always possible."

71

He insisted that the visitors leave immediately, and since they were, in fact, his guests they did as he bade them.

Making their goodbyes in the doorway, all the visitors must have surely felt they were betraying their own intentions in coming to Nicaragua in the first place, but they went anyway, feeling that to resist their insistent guide would do little but provoke acrimony.

Just as they were going down the walk the machine shop next door began to whine, and yammer, and shake. A high-pitched squeal issued forth. It seemed as though the Vegas' flimsy tin roof might come flying off.

"Our Revolution never sleeps," said their guide. "It never even takes a proper *siesta.*"

"Heavens," the young Swede.

"Surely not," his elder colleague responded with a joke. "It's just the roof."

The ground beneath them shook.

"The gods must be very mad at us though," the older Swede added. From his tiny wooden verandah, Patricio Vegas called out, "Now you know how we feel. Now you know . . ."

"Don't pay any attention to that trouble-maker," young Perra said. Patricio said, "He lives in a mansion in La Colonia with the rest of his cell. They have a cook and a VCR. While we . . ."

"Shut up," young Perra said.

"Now you know how we feel," Patricio added. "Now you finally know."

The world beneath them shuddered one more time.

Young Perra shrugged. "With such roosters we make soup."

"With such oxen they govern," Patricio cried out. But the Swedes were already seated in their jeep, were driving off into the dust of the long hot afternoon.●

ON CREDIT (1981)

The letter from the bank manager was polite, even somewhat diffident about repayment: "Please try to see me or one of my assistants in the next couple of days."

Such gentle treatment surprised Arturo Calvo. He was a month overdue on a loan to purchase airline tickets with dollars so his daughter Rima could leave the country to join her husband in Miami.

In his commonplace book he observed, "This government surprises like the behavior of an over-active child. You expect mischief and receive fair play and then you are not prepared for ill treatment when it happens in the future."

Calvo was hardly a poor man by Nicaraguan standards. In *cordobas* the sum he owed was easily manageable, but the bank wanted to be paid back, as it had paid out — in dollars — more than Calvo had, or he wouldn't have borrowed in the first place. There had been no coffee harvest last winter and he'd been forced to sell cattle to the state to survive, and now he was in a very precarious condition. The state, through the bank, held quite a bit of his land as collateral; he owed his housekeeper two month's wages and was permitting her and her family to live in the west wing of the *finca* as a payment of sorts.

That he'd become untrustworthy from a fiduciary point of view was not appealing to Calvo.

He was a graduate of Texas A&M, and he'd built his holdings in Nicaragua through his own exertions. It was humiliating to be, in his words, "a deadbeat."

Calvo believed in credit. Credit was the basis of all human understanding. He understood why the state had come to supplant his bankers in the New Nicaragua, and he had no doubt he was at fault. In former times he'd always lent money to his tenants and expected prompt repayment. If he didn't want to lose his property, Calvo observed, he would have to come up with family money or a new partner, preferably the former.

As Arturo Calvo tried to button the sleeve on his stiff white *guayabera* shirt he noticed a second button was missing. He'd have to get la Señora, as he called her out of respect, to sew for him. Meantime, he was very late for his Rotary luncheon, and afterwards he was meeting Cousin Ima at the National Cemetery to visit his wife's grave. They did this once a month and the last time there'd been an invasion alert and the visit was cancelled. Calvo had tender feelings for Ima, even more so. He also felt she would understand his feelings, and by understanding him could be a help, one way or the other.

Lately, he felt so isolated with his troubles. Going into the kitchen, he found his usual small white cup of black coffee set out for him and swallowed it quickly, like medicine, in a couple of gulps.

"God will help you put a master loan together," la Señora told him when he discussed his troubles with her the evening before. "You're a good man, a good boss. God can't fail you, Señor."

La Señora was Pentecostal. She believed in miracles. The trouble was he didn't. When he told her about his collateral problems, she said, "The work here is important to Him. Praise the Lord. He will want to help you."

Calvo finished his coffee and scribbled a note to his housekeeper: "You need not wait up to serve me. I will take something in the city."

Then he went back to his room to find the bank letter. He'd telephone from Managua and see if he couldn't stall the manager.

Beyond the ramada three old cars were parked in single file. All three were Swedish makes, Volvos and Saabs, and he hung onto them to cannibalize spare parts for a fourth bullet-riddled Volvo sedan which he kept parked in the alleyway to the side of the house. The Volvo was bottle-green and had come with many deluxe features, such as air conditioning and a CB radio, but now it could drive only in low gears and burned up large quantities of oil.

Calvo initially blamed its sluggishness on the Soviet gasoline, a staple of all Nicaraguan transport since the U.S. trade sanctions, but he was assured by a right-wing mechanic that the gas was of very high quality, equal to that of Pemex or Exxon. The problem was with his gearbox, a stray bullet, and no replacements available.

It was a bulky, green, impressive-looking vehicle, if you didn't look too closely. Its leather seats long since had rotted away and were replaced with old pillows covered with bright red kitchen oilcloth. Calvo used the car a lot. As an agronomist, he merited a gasoline allowance of about ten gallons a week, but, to stretch his reserves, he added alcohol distilled from his own sugar cane, and he also had attached metal coils calculated to conduct the resulting vapors through the valves back to the engine.

When Calvo travelled he was accompanied by loud coughs and farts and sputters, though he usually arrived at his destination, after a while. As his noisy locomotion wasn't very different from that of most Nicaraguans, he was paid little heed. He tried hard not to break any laws; but he was conspicuous enough.

"You are like Joseph in Egypt," Ima once told him. He saw himself as more sadly vexed than any mere hostage. His productivity, he believed, allowed the regime to oppress him all the more. What were the alternatives? There was talk of the state paying him in dollars for his produce, instead of all those worthless *cordobas,* but if he did not continue to produce, he would almost surely lose his farms.

In town, Calvo hurried to the small suite of offices he shared with several other private growers and called his bank manager, who, though an old family friend, was now an employee of the state.

"Nothing to be done," the fellow said. "You don't pay and you are stealing from the People. No matter what you and I may think, I can only try to slow things down for you with paper work."

Calvo said he was grateful, but he didn't wish to cause his friend any trouble. He offered to assign his Volvo as further collateral on the loan. The manager accepted. He rarely took in anything as nice as a working Volvo junker.

"May I say," he told Calvo, "You are a true *hidalgo.*"

·"That's not in great demand these days," Calvo reminded him.

The Rotary luncheon was held, as always, at Managua's foremost *churrasco* steak restaurant. It was a garish open-air pit beneath a vined ramada, tile floors thick with sawdust. There were brightly checked tablecloths and photos of bullfighters, boxers, and ballplayers. The business crowd preferred this place to the hotels, as it was only a few blocks from the Plaza de España.

On the way to his table, Calvo met his cousin, Gil Rosas, who worked for the government in military procurement. Their mothers were sisters but he and Gil were never very close; Rosas had lived abroad for many years and only returned after the Victory. He now claimed to be solicitous about Calvo's affairs. Was he managing to get by?

"It's nice of you to ask," Calvo said, as though to dismiss the subject.

"If I can ever intervene," Rosas said. "After all, blood . . . "

"As you say," Calvo replied, with a little bow, and went off to his Rotarian friends.

There were three less present today and Calvo easily figured out that the absent were the latest to emigrate. He nodded at all those who were in attendance and, since the meal was already in progress, took an empty place at the long table next to his old school chum, Mejia Martinez.

Mejia Martinez was a man of considerable cunning. While nobody's spy or operative, he always managed to find high-paying employment, in currency other than *cordobas,* with foreign companies. Now he was the agent for a British fishing consortium on the East Coast, and patronized the dollar stores.

He was a slim man with a burnt dark face and he always wore tinted glasses, though Calvo could recall how, at the Salesian school at Masaya, he had been fair and blue-eyed, just like a little Englishman, or a German.

He was on his third wife, a young Swedish beauty he kept in San José, and two of his children had died in 1979 in the street fighting in Estelí and Managua. For his friend, Calvo, he always showed a warm smile and many effusive words, though he was known to be a bitter, sardonic man. Today his friendliness was definitely tinged with sardonicism.

"We're the last of the rats here, old boy. The ship already has its keel up I'm afraid." He gripped Calvo by the shoulder and squeezed. "What do you say to that?"

"If saying made a difference," Calvo said, as though to mock him.

The waiter brought him his steak.

· He was warned it would probably be a bit overdone and a little cold, and Calvo nodded and avowed he would take any kind of beer in place of the raw rum punch.

From across the way Gutierez, of the Victoria Brewery, said, "If you drink government piss you'll piss government piss."

"We are all increasingly optimistic these days," Calvo replied.

The chair gaveled them to rise and they sang the opening song:

"The eyes of Texas are upon you
all the live long day . . ."

Calvo had quite forgotten how many of his business friends had been at Texas A&M with him, or even before him.

Afterwards Costa of Algodones Tipitapa spoke on "marketing in a semi-socialist economy."

"For our own sakes," he said, "and the honor of our pocketbooks, we must continue to regard our efforts as the single most productive aspect of this mobilized state. If we nourish it with our labor and initiative, it will surely nourish us in years to come. We are entering a new phase in this century, of perhaps political as well as economic democracy. But the Party will have the same right, and they will exercise it in the farms as well as in the factories. Look around you," he added. "Are there any state informers here? Only businessmen, like you and me, the stalwarts of the republic."

It was well known by all that Costa was a Party member and when he finished speaking, all the men gladly broke up into small groups and talked: gossip, taxes, prices, dollars, expropriations. Calvo drifted from group to group and finally found himself chatting with Armando Reiss, who'd left the priesthood at the time of the Revolution to take over his father's bristle firm. Reiss was a strict stout sallow little man who wore a goatee under his chin and kept his steel gray hair chopped short. He was said to be a notorious lecher "with either sex," and it was also rumored he was well connected to the Borge faction of the regime.

They were smoking together when Reiss suddenly asked, "Have you bought your plane tickets yet?"

It was that sort of provocative question Reiss was always asking—as though he hoped to trap Calvo into some kind of admission.

Even if Calvo had a ticket in his pocket he doubted he would confess it to Reiss, so he shrugged and backed away from him—to drift from group to group, aimlessly. Even if he went away, Calvo was hoping to return every few months to keep title to his properties, as the law required.

When he saw nobody was watching him, he went out the door to go to the cemetery. He might be early but he would surely be unmolested among the monuments of the dead.

He parked alongside the church and entered through the main wrought-iron gates where peddlers were holding out flowers, colored ices for sucking, and handbills of printed prayers. Calvo dropped some coins for a legless beggar and walked past everybody else to stand, for a moment, among the aisles of black and rose and gray-blue marble and granite tombs.

The place was well shaded from the leafy limbs of some large almond trees and the air was cool. He was again chagrined to note where vandals shortly after the Revolution pulled down all the monuments of the tyrant and his family.

Every time he came to this familiar site it was as though the vacancy of the rows of empty crypts was a sort of monument. During the tyrant's time a brown soldier, fifteen feet high in battle dress, stood with his rifle at present arms above the crypts of Somozas, DeBayles, and Portacarreros.

The first days of the Revolution levelled all that, as though a bulldozer went prowling through the tombs, and all was now returned to vacancy.

Calvo thought of how his dead wife had come down in the world of her own estimations. When they'd known she was going to die, she made him promise to arrange for her burial in the National Cemetery, among her distinguished relatives. Calvo obliged, despite the fact that it was costly. Now she lay eternally in a place of shame.

The section where Graciella was interred was familiarly called by some old families "St. Tropez," and was much favored by them because it was a broad hillside with a view of the old cathedral and the ruined city below. The architecture here was decidedly classical and European: capitals and pediments, crypts with marble, and brass posts. Calvo walked out along the iron fence and sat down on a stone bench in a section barely occupied by any graves, where a grove of citrus trees recently had been planted. He could see all of the traffic pass in and out of the cemetery gates from here and remain inconspicuous.

By turning his head, Calvo could also watch a funeral in progress on the other side of the grove, in the small bare Potter's field which had been established many years back for family retainers. The figures of the mourners, among knee-high weeds and discarded trash, seemed graven and scored, as in medieval drawings. Calvo could feel his own history here, and it was not all shameful to him, but coherent, almost palpable, despite these various desecrations. He thought it was not as odd to be sitting here like this, as it had seemed all day long among his colleagues.

Chimes tolled the hour. His eyes roved the cemetery for Ima, or perhaps other friends who'd come to visit their loved ones.

Behind his back he heard loud harsh weeping and dared not turn around to look at the woman who was so upset. Then an official limousine drove up and an army officer emerged, exchanged salutes with the two guards at the main gate, who were at present arms, and went back into his car and was driven off again.

It was getting hotter and Calvo opened the top buttons on his *guayabera*. He felt as though he could doze, but forced himself to stay awake.

He saw Cousin Ima enter through a door in the gate that adjoined the sanctuary of the church. She'd been at prayer, and now she carried a bouquet of flowers for the grave, down the avenues of tombs.

Ima was some years younger than Calvo and still quite well-off. When he saw her, the flame in him sputtered up. His pulse quickened; he sometimes stammered a little in her presence. She looked so much like his wife, except that Graciella had never been so elegant or pretty. Ima seemed to seize people's attentions whenever she walked into a room. She was slim and tall, with fair skin and very dark hair. She moved like a reed in the wind.

Coming toward him now, following a sightless path his way, as though she could not see him but was drawn to his direction, Ima seemed like the most casual of mourners. She wore stylish black jeans and new white beach sneakers, a black short-sleeved blouse like some fashion mannequin might wear, to emphasize her bosoms. She was thirty and a mother, but she could have passed for an undergraduate. He often marvelled at what good fortune had provoked him to choose her as his confidant. When she walked past his place on the bench inside the grove, not noticing him, he got up and followed her.

They'd originally agreed to meet like this, over Graciella's grave, to make plans for the future, as each was dissatisfied with the regime and with life in present-day Nicaragua. (Ima's husband was a magistrate of no particular distinction except that he was known to be a philanderer of wide-ranging proclivities.) Within a month, a sort of love, or passion, for each other seized them both, and was acknowledged — the ache to touch, the desire to be lovers. They only went as far as they could in a cemetery. Once, he'd led her behind a huge Sacasa memorial and they'd kissed in long gulps, and even more, with Calvo's back to the raised letters of family deceased.

Calvo invested all his hopes in Ima. They would love and save each other.

Calvo also believed he loved Ima enough that he wanted to take her out of the country to live with him, but when she turned suddenly and saw him behind her on the path, her look seemed more sad than surprised. She actually seemed frightened of him for suddenly appearing like that.

"What's the matter, Ima dear?" he asked, reaching for her hands, but she drew back, away from him. "What is it child?" He liked to call her that. "It can't be that bad," he urged her. "Tell me."

"I only know I love you," she said, but she had such a pale sick look on her face as she spoke.

They'd stopped near a small patch of children's tombs. She was looking at the ground, as though she'd just confessed to something shameful.

"What could be wrong with love between the two of us?" Calvo asked. "Why is that something to worry about?"

She shook her head at him, but said nothing.

"What?" he demanded. "Tell me."

"José Antonio knows." Softly, she was peering up at him from under her coif. "He has asked only for me not to bring him dishonor among his friends."

Calvo grinned. If it was only that, he was truly relieved.

"It's about time," he told her. "So we'll leave now, won't we. It can't really matter to anybody else . . ."

"I'm pregnant again," she declared. "It won't be so easy."

"I shall be happy to say I'm the father." he announced.

"No, that can't be, and you know that."

"Nevertheless," he told her, "I will be the child's father. Praise God."

Calvo thought he wanted people to believe the child was his — even so.

"He'll want the child," Ima explained, weakly, "because it will keep me here."

It was as though the effort to give such explanations was taxing to her. Calvo felt he had to reassure Ima, that it was her sense of being so vulnerable, so ill-at-ease, which made him anxious.

He took her hand and led her over to Graciella's small, well-tended grave and stood with her there, silently, a moment. He supposed the way they stood was only making her more fretful. What if somebody should see them like this?

Calvo kept his voice low. "If you must stay then I will too—to be with you.

"You must leave," she said. "It's no good for you at all to be here."

"I am certainly unhappy," Calvo said, "but I am not disloyal to you or the state. I will stay because I must if you must."

Later Calvo would reflect that he'd never really wished to leave Nicaragua and was only making the invitation because he did not wish Ima to go without him.

If that was so, it was also true that with his head bowed, and standing over his wife's grave, he could hardly look ahead.

They stood that way a long time, holding hands together, and Calvo was crying, and she seemed calmer outwardly, though roiling within.

Their silence settled on them like a soft rain until, at last, she turned and pecked him on the cheek: It was late and she was expected home to look after the baby.

Alone then, Calvo spoke to his dead wife: "You know I am doing the right thing. I cannot leave Nicaragua without you or her."

He knew he was telling a lie, but Graciella was dead and she could hardly care. He was close to a truth of sorts.

He started away from the grave. The life he had left him was small; he'd be joining Graciella soon enough. Meantime Ima would be needing him here, and he her. He would not ask Ima to help him right away. But perhaps, later, she would, if he stayed on.

As he went through the cemetery gates, Calvo stopped to purchase a bag of sweets from a child with a ruined foot. He usually didn't like sweet things, but it was time to get over all his old aversions. The woman he loved was pregnant by her husband. She preferred it that way. He gave a beggar a coin and told her to pray for him. The little things in life can make such a big difference, he thought. ●

"Those are the roads
  where we go to serve the
    Christians;
  and even though we worked
    hard
  we turn at the end of some time
  to our houses
  and our women
  and our children;
  though now we're going off
    without hope
  of ever more turning back,
  nor of seeing them, of having
    more children."

Lament of the Chorotegas, quoted by
Bartolomeo De La Casas, who translated
it from the Nahuatl language for his
Destruction of the Indians, 1552

PART 2

IN TIPITAPA (1979)

In early September, in the early morning, the small children are in the fields "cleaning" cotton plants. They look like little Arabs, bundled up in sarapes, or in some cases towels and bedsheets, against the dust and the occasional low-flying crop sprayers. Their overseers are grown men and a few women who walk among them like arrogant giants. All around stretch dark green fields of crops and an endless echoing blue sky, cloudless except when a plane comes in low to spray.

There are just as many girls as boys, and some mothers who seem to be supervising the work of their children; row by row, they all have to get down on their knees to do the work, pressing themselves into the hot thorny earth.

Every couple of hours a break is called; some bring jars of water, plastic bags of coke or *cacao,* food. They eat huddled over their food in small groups, and they never take much because what they took with them is meant to last the whole day.

In the afternoon the sun is hottest and they work choking in the dust their feet make, and are regularly reproached by their overseers. These reproaches are like those of relatives, gentle enough though annoying: one is not being thorough, neglecting the stems of the plants. As the afternoon wears on, the children receive more and more reproaches and they grow more and more cranky. Some doze off; others gossip idly and do nothing.

At last open trucks arrive from Tipitapa and the children are paid off in coins and small bills by their labor contractors and are helped aboard. The overseers sit in the cabs with the drivers. They all are jouncing back to town.

The first thing the children do is buy more soda for themselves from one of the market women.

Then some of the older boys go off to play pool while the children hurry home to bring money to their mothers so they can shop for supper. There is very little worth buying in the marketplace. The cotton cloths for which Tipitapa was once famous are no longer being woven.

Some of the grown men stand in front of a tavern waiting for a friend to come along with money to buy them drinks. Their faces are as dark as the earth and cracked from the sun in places. In front of a big church some militia are being taught the manual of arms. They have army blankets at their feet as though they will shortly be field-stripping their weapons.

Some police come off their shifts at the "Model Prison" and enter the saloon. A man rides into town on a fancy high saddle over a small Chontales pony. Some women appear with shopping bags.

The principal street of Tipitapa looks like a wash, lined with dark boulders, in the late sun. The men stay on; they have no motion left to them. They will stay through the oncoming darkness. They will think about the morning and how they will try to pass the time then. They will be here to watch their children go off to the fields. They will search for friends. They will complain to each other: Will there be another war? Dark now and the men are still standing there . . .●

NICARAGUA AND THE JEWISH PROBLEM (1981)

"Seen any elephants around here recently?" Prudhomme asked.

He was sitting by the hotel pool drinking black coffee.

"Not so I would notice," I told him. "Just the usual snakes."

"But soon you will," he told me. "Never fear—and in the ballroom."

He got up from his chair and led me to the ballroom, where a press conference was commencing. Some people from the Ministry of the Interior were leading in a swarthy, balding man with a prominent nose, Minister Levitas of the government Tourism Office, a Minister without much of a Ministry since few tourists as such came to Nicaragua, and those who did picked coffee or helped with the "alphabetization" campaign, and were handled by functionaries of the FSLN or through the wife of Ortega, Rosario Murillo.

The Minister was surrounded by a small knot of press. He raised his hands to speak: "As a Jew of Jewish descent I wish to speak out against the calumny that this government is anti-Semitic. If it were I would know for sure. My own brother died fighting for the FSLN; they named a bus station after him."

A woman from UPI asked if the Minister considered himself "observant."

"Not exactly, but I am not prohibited from being so."

He smiled at the Interior people by his side, as though about to present them with a large unsecured loan or, perhaps, a paper at an international conference on the status of the elephant. "I am not alone," he said. "There is also the poetess Nachlis."

"There have been complaints made by B'nai Brith and other American groups," a network reporter declared. "What do you say to them? And to the former Jews of Nicaragua in Miami who say they have been dispossessed."

"Only if they collaborated with the old regime," Levitas said. "There were never many full Jews in Nicaragua but there are many half and quarter Jews even in this government — the poet Cardenal, for example."

"He is a priest — *Catolico*," a man from Interior corrected him.

"But his great-grandfather . . ." said Levitas.

"Never mind Cardenal," he was told. "Stick to here and now."

"Do you see an elephant anywhere, Mr. Minister?" asked Prudhomme.

"I don't get your point."

Prudhomme said, "In order for there to be a Jewish problem there should be elephants, I believe."

The Minister swallowed air: "I am anti-Zionist. I do not deny that . . . Israelis are gangsters. They supplied Somoza . . ."

"With elephants," Prudhomme interjected.

He led me out to the patio where an urn of coffee had been placed and some of the press were already refreshing themselves.

"Brother," he said, "do you really care? I don't. A certain anti-Semitism seems requisite throughout the third world to remind them of what they lack in large measure — namely Jews."

"I'm from a Jewish family," I said. "So is the Minister, I suppose."

"It means nothing to me." Prudhomme shrugged and disengaged himself from my shadow. He stood by the pool peering down into the chlorinated blue water.

Presently the Minister and his two companions came outside and joined us. They said, "You must have questions you would like answered."

I had no questions.

"I have many friends in the States," the Minister said, "some relatives."

"I'm sure," I told him.

"You have Jewish blood?" he asked, his voice suddenly husky.

I whispered back, "Indeed."

"So," said one of the government men, "you can see we are not bad anti-Semites when we make a Jew a cabinet minister."

"Absolutely, I have no doubts," I said.

Prudhomme rejoined us. He poked at my ribs. "Mr. Minister, this fellow here is your co-religionist."

"I'm certain of it." The Minister was grinning.

"Aumein sela halleluyah," I said.

"Please gentlemen," he said.

He shook both our hands and turned as if to go.

The Interior man said, "He's going to make a TV broadcast to Canada."

"Next year in Montreal," I said.

"Please," said the Minister.

Prudhomme said, "Pass me an elephant."

"Please. Help yourself," said the Minister.

I said, *"Azoy . . ."*

And the next thing I knew we were all three standing outside the hotel in blinding white sunlight glare.

The two government people went to fetch their car.

"It's a shame we haven't more time to talk," the Minister said.

"Not really," I said. "But good luck . . . good luck anyway," I added.

"Maybe we will someday," he said.

"I doubt it, frankly," I added.

The car pulled up.

"Call me sometime," the Minister said, like a woman leaving the apartment of the man she'd just spent the night with.

Prudhomme said, "We are always glad to speak with Jewish ministers."

Levitas sat in the back with his two bodyguards in the front, and the sedan lurched when it started, and drove off into the steaming midday sun. ●

DO YOU SEE ANY PORTERS ANYWHERE? (1984)

At the *hacienda* outside Ocatal, after the battle, the Chief of State came to talk to the people. He tried to be consoling even though there were five dead and more wounded.

"We are a nation at war against powerful malevolent forces," he said. "But we have many friends beyond our borders, and the world applauds our courage and determination."

People wept, and cried out names of the dead who were laid out under tarps, like produce, in the principal square, awaiting burial later in the day.

Across the way, I stood next to Prudhomme, who was actually making notes on a small pad with a little mechanical pencil.

"Is any of this new to you?" I asked.

"Not really," he confessed.

I asked why he bothered to make notes.

"He is, after all, the Chief of State," Prudhomme said, "and those are corpses . . . whether new to me or not."

His eyes were very watery.

Afterwards he dragged me up past the security guard toward the man himself. "Ask him a question," Prudhomme demanded. I had no questions. "You ask," I said.

Prudhomme waved at the man and caught his glance. "It's good that you came," he said.

The Chief of State waved back.

"That's no question," I said.

"I haven't any questions to ask" he said flatly.

Two days later near Paradise, Honduras, we listened to a similar speech from Calero to a bunch of new Contra recruits, mostly kids it seemed, from the East Coast.

He's a heavy-set man with a saturnine smile, and I could not say his speech was any less affecting than Ortega's. Well fed himself, he fed all those puny kids, sweating inside heavy green fatigues, words: that the time was coming when Nicaragua was going to be liberated and freedom was going to be restored. Later they were served beans and G.I. rations.

Again Prudhomme took notes and before I could ask why he told me. "In order to put some distance between myself and pathos," he said. "One side or the other. It's always like that when people are dying . . ."

There were the remains of a *fiesta* in the next village and we walked about among the stalls and watched a cockfight. Prudhomme put some money down on a large fellow with white feathers. Before we knew it he was a mess of blood. Lifeless, a rag.

A one-eyed man told us we should bet on Dario, his cock, next, because he fed him special marijuana seeds and the bird was "crazy in a good way when it comes to cocks."

We walked on.

"Don't you think," my friend asked when we stopped to buy Cokes, "that people who live like this have wars like this?"

"Europe and America are still pretty bloodthirsty," I said.

"Drink your Coke," he said. "It's getting late."

On the plane back to Managua we sat next to an Asian businessman who called himself Micky. He said he sold commercial fishing equipment for a Singapore trading firm.

Prudhomme asked, "What sort of equipment?"

"For catching fish," Micky said.

"What sort of fish?" I asked.

"Typical fish." He was a thin man, impeccably dressed in a dark rayon suit, a white shirt, a red tie, as though preparing to go on TV. The frames of his eyeglasses were thick dark tortoise shell.

"Do you plan to sell your typical fishing equipment in Managua?" Prudhomme asked.

The man grinned.

"Not at all," he said, "Our company also has this sideline . . ."

"What sort of sideline?" Prudhomme asked.

"Typical sideline," he said.

Prudhomme asked, "You don't wish to specify?"

Micky replied, "Weaponry . . . It's all very State of the Art."

He asked who we worked for. "We are *pomps funebres,*" Prudhomme said, "a sort of joint undertaking."

Micky turned to me. "Does your journalist friend always tell such bad jokes?"

"Sometimes he just chases yellowtail," I said.

When our plane landed Micky was met by another Oriental wearing a *guayabera,* who helped him pass quickly through customs.

Prudhomme waved goodbye. *"Vaya con Visa, Micky,"* he called after them.

Our bags were examined by a former police officer. Prudhomme said, "I thought you were now living in Miami."

"You're thinking of a different policeman," the man said when he put a chalk mark on my typewriter case.

There was a brisk trade for dollars nearby. People were moving about; somebody had just arrived in the VIP Lounge. I told the customs man I thought he was lucky they hadn't made him the porter.

All of a sudden, he put his hands on his hips and hollered at me: "Do you see any porters anywhere?" His face was full of sweat. "If you see any porters anywhere," he said, "you should help yourselves." He stamped his foot.

We took a cab into town. A couple of lorries passed us full of militia moving north.

"Typical lorries?" Prudhomme said.

"Typical," our driver said.

He then asked if we would pay him in dollars. "Typical fish." I asked. "Typical!" Prudhomme laughed.

Prudhomme paid the driver. I took the bags.

A buzzard flung its wings at the dead blue sky above us. ●

TURNABOUT (1984)

The informer was called a patriot by everybody except the people who knew him best in his own neighborhood; they called him simply "the Ear." This insult was double because that was what informers were called during the hated years of the Tyranny. But those days of intimidation were said to be long over. Jesús Galabos' neighbors, nevertheless, liked to point out he was a member of the SDN, and was only doing his duty when reporting bits and pieces of unruly speech and behavior to his contact in the Ministry of the Interior. It wasn't like the old days really; those people had been so depraved.

Jesús was a small dark man with over-eager brown eyes which stared constantly out at the world from beneath his great domed bald head. He was perhaps the only person in his *barrio* who'd lived in the hated U.S.A. So he would say he knew all its vices and evils. Galabos had made his living once as a shrimp fisherman in Puerto Peñasco, Sonora, and then for a while he was a "coyote," ferrying aliens across the border from Mexicali for a good price and, as often as not, bringing them to the Border Patrol.

"They don't love brown people in the States. They don't love anybody but the rich. So I did what I was paid to do, and the Border Patrol also paid, from time to time."

He was sixty. He looked both wizened and sleek, as fit as a man of only fifty perhaps. His wife, who knew all his habits, lived with him but would not "cohabit," under the instructions of her priest. All his life he'd been a hungry man and even when he had gone to pains to satisfy that hunger it still gnawed at him. So now he'd chosen to work for the state which, alone, in Nicaragua could sate his needs.

He found he was more surprised than he might have imagined when the lives of his neighbors were affected by the things he told his contacts. People were suddenly prey to his whims: a printer had his hours changed, a housewife was disciplined for claiming more household members than she had; a brewery worker was accused of malingering. He visited his slanders, without prejudice, on everybody alike.

So many things were happening to the friends and neighbors of Galabos that people started to shun him, and he had to go further afield to supply his weekly bounty of anti-social behavior. He did so, nevertheless, out of a feeling of near omnipotence. Never before had he seemed so much the master over others, and consequently over himself. To himself he was *"Muy estimado Galabos,"* though, in fact, he was not even a proper civil servant.

One day he went to call at noontime at the house of an old *cumpa,* Juan Kino. When he climbed the rickety porch steps and peered in through the window of the front room, he saw Kino's pretty wife, Linda, naked beneath the dark thrusting hairy body of a thickset man who was definitely not Juan. Galabos backed away and thanked his stars he'd been quiet, discreet. He would put the matter to the back of his mind. But that Sunday afternoon, at the Star Bar, he found himself telling the incident to his handler, whom he couldn't help noticing was also dark and thickset, with a wiry full beard like Fidel's.

"Adultery in the front room. Only fancy," the man said. "Did you see the fellow's face?"

"I'm not sure," Galabos said.

"Do you think you could identify him?"

"Surely," he replied. "That will never be necessary. It was only sin."

"I asked you a question," his handler insisted sternly. And his eyes blinked hard. "Yes?"

"Surely no," Galabos lied. "Surely I could be mistaken and all that . . ."

"We shall see."

The man from the Ministry scribbled something in his little note pad. "We lie for so many different reasons we never understand the reasons why we lie," he said, and dismissed Jesús, urging him to be more diligent, and truthful.

Jesús went away with small trepidations. When, a few days later, he was told he was going to be disciplined for filing "untruthful reports," he was still incredulous. "It's too late in life for this," he said.

"It's a mistake to think," he reflected, in his new job in a flour warehouse, "that by admitting to lies we are being truthful."

His hair was now white with flour dust.

"It's a mistake to think one can decide these things oneself . . . a mistake to think . . ."●

MANAGUA 4:30 P.M (1978)

"y si he de dar un testimonio sobre mi epoca es este: Fue barbara y primitiva pero poetica"

("If I had to testify about my age I would say: it was barbarous and primitive but poetic.")

Ernesto Cardenal, "Managua 6:30 P.M."

In Managua in September 1978, at the cat house called The Witch, Sophy, a young whore, told me, "I should get one of those pallet mattresses such as the peddlers sell and the people use. Then I could take my business to the soldiers in the street."

She was pale and pretty with dark hair, doll-like, and small-breasted; and she was very angry she wasn't seeing any of her best customers any more. Some of her customers were the best people in Nicaragua. She said she had been used by some of Managua's leading middle class doctors, engineers, civil servants and military men, even *los pacos* (the police), with and without her good friend Alma, the fake blonde; and she truly resented the disuse to which she had been put of late by the curfew, the state of martial law, and the contact bombs at night.

Because I did not wish to sleep with her and had only given her forty *cordobas* as a tip for talking to me, she claimed she was also very very hungry and would talk much better in the Hotel Intercontinental dining rooms.

"I don't wish to feed you," I said.

"Why not?" She wiggled her little hips, and there were two blush marks on her pale smooth waxy cheeks. "I am very hungry."

"Because you are not my type."

"Then you would like my friend *la rubia*," Sophy said. "Alma . . ."

"I don't think so. Not now."

Sophy glanced at me suspiciously. The truth was I had
no desire, and she was too petite, too childlike, and cold. I
knew she would be frightened of me.

"You got the jitters?" Sophy asked. "A doctor examined
my pussy the day of Matagalpa and I was declared
healthy."

"Bravo," I said. "It's not that."

Then she said all the foreign press who had come to
Nicaragua to cover this war were sissies and the women
reporters were all bitches, dykes. She also said she was
very good and I would see if only I would let her come
with me, or we could do it right here, with Alma, who was
a little bit taller than she was and had nipples that I would
surely like to take into my mouth and suck.

The image of those little pink nipples hardened me a
moment, and then I drifted off into my own numb self-
righteousness again: I just couldn't go with Sophy, even
though I knew she was very hungry. It would be like talking dirty with my daughter: embarrassing, funny.

Sophy's face turned solemn. She wondered why I had
come to Nicaragua.

"To learn about the people," I said, "and the war."

"You did not come to make *che che?*" she asked,
peevishly.

"Really it doesn't matter," I assured her. "That sort of
thing is everywhere; when one wants to have it one can
have it easily. I don't wish to take your time. But I do wish
to talk."

"Talk of what?"

"About your customers," I said, and lied a little in addi-
tion: "I heard you were the fanciest whore in all of
Managua . . . and the best . . . for a story I would even pay
you."

"Yes, clearly," she went.

Nodding slowly with her small perfect oval face, she
leaned toward me then, and spoke with an ever increasing

earnestness: "I will tell you a story. People say the Somozas are bad. They are only saying what they heard others say. I know.

"Before the battles I used to go dancing every night in the week when I wasn't working with my boyfriend at the Frisco Disco. You know the place? It was not too far from here in Managua, only they burned it down, *los rebeldes,* because it was owned by some Somoza people."

Sophy pronounced her *z*s softly, like *ths,* as Spaniards do, and every time she waited to see if I would notice how classy she sounded.

Then she said, "The brother of this general from Masaya, he owned it and he had lived in your country and that is why Norberto called it Frisco Disco."

"That was a very nice place, with a lotta lights and good music, and all the best people would come there. Somotha's son, *el mayor,* Tachito, he would come there, too, and once they said Bianca Yagger of the Rolling Stones, when she came to visit with her family here, but I didn't see her there so I don't really know.

"So one night I am just with Rudolfo my boy friend and we are both very tired because we have been fucking all the time, all night long and all day, too, on this big holiday in Holy Week, and was a lot of work, you know, and we just wanted to take it easy and dance, you know . . ."

She grinned at me for approval. When I grinned back she took one of my cigarettes off the end table, lit up, and went on.

Sophy said, "In the middle of the floor is this man he is one of my customers, and he is there with his daughter, and I am embarrassed for him — you know — and I don't want to say anything because even those things can happen and I say to my Rudolfo don't look you . . .

"So we are just dancing in the lights when this man he sees me and he is a very rich man, and *pues,* he wants to talk. We should come home with him and his daughter, and all make love together but I don't want to because I am so tired and I wish to be all alone tonight with Rudolfo; and I don't think it is such a good thing to do anyway . . . a father and his daughter.

"He has an awful lot of dollars this man and he will give me $100 if we will come with him, and Rudolfo, I know, will be angry with me if I say no so I'm saying yes I think so but first I must go to pee pee. You know . . .

"Because I am afraid I am bleeding and that would not be so nice for all concerned.

"When I come back Rudolfo is there with the daughter, and the man, I will call him Jonas, dances with me and then he becomes very intimate with me on the dance floor and he says his daughter wants *me* very much, too, and that is why we are going and he is paying so much money because it is her birthday.

"I look at this girl he calls his daughter and she is not so pretty, but she is clearly his daughter. Well I think I could do worse. A woman is so easy, and soft . . .

"So we go home with them, the two of us, and it is like always, you know, and afterwards I am so disgusted with what has happened I call them both *vos*. I refuse to be familiar with them, and I tell Rudolfo, 'Never again.' That is what we do here in Nicaragua: to use the impersonal, you know?"

"I know."

"It was Rudolfo who had the girl the second time after me and he give her too much pleasure so I try with her again because I have to know how he is feeling with her, and I think that way, you know your house is my house, as we say.

"But . . . with the man," she added, abruptly, "I have had not too much pleasure because I don't like his breath.

"So afterwards," Sophy shrugged, weakly, "we went home and slept and I had such a bad headache in the morning because we took all this cocaine. You know," she added again, "those were, how you say, 'good old days' over here in Managua."

I asked, "When was that?"

"Before the *terremoto.*"

"1972?"

"Even before. Lots fun! I was very young."

"And since?"

"The same. Every night in the week. You call that fun?"

Sophy was giggling at me, as if spoofing our seriousness together. Her face, all red and slightly sweaty, seemed very childlike.

Something about her animation touched me. If it was sex it was also something else, too: she seemed alive for the first time since we'd begun to talk.

I asked, "Why did that man have so much money? What did he do?"

She thought a moment, her brow wrinkled.

"He was just a Jew."

"Just?"

"He sold *things,*" she said, "to the army, and he had cotton and race horses. A Turk, a Jew, an Arab—I didn't know."

"And now?"

"Maybe he is in the Coconut Grove, Miami, with all the others."

She smirked mischievously.

"And his daughter?"

"She is just Rudolfo's whore but she is no good, I tell you, because she likes girls. They please her more."

She seemed angry, and then bemused.

I said I was sorry if she had lost her pimp to some rich man's daughter.

"It's the same with me," she shrugged. "Once I liked Rudolfo. Now I no longer care for such people."

"Do you have another?"

"*Claro,* because now I do it only for the money." Sophy caught her lip between her teeth: "And for you, for love . . ."

She was coquettish again, blinking her long greasy black eyelashes.

"I would suck you dry," she said, huskily, "if you would only let me."

"So you're thirsty as well as hungry?"

"I want to make *jeeg-jeeg* with your *pelotas.*"

She made a motion with her hand as if she were bouncing a ball, and then she said, "I say *pelotas* because *cojones* is for anybody — a *campesino.* No?"

I asked, "How did the disco burn?"

Disappointed with me, Sophy said, "Maybe it deserved to happen."

"I guess others thought so."

"I could put my tongue into your asshole," Sophy said.

She wasn't smiling any more. Sophy really seemed to want me and it was not for business alone. She wanted somebody, a man, because she was hungry, and frightened of being alone, and she didn't know what to expect if the rebels seized power.

I couldn't insult her.

"If we go to the room could we just hug each other and be gentle? No funny stuff?" I hoped I was expressing her feelings equally.

"You know," I told her, "I've seen so many cadavers the last few days, I'm not sure I'm feeling at all sexy."

"You will talk dirty to me," Sophy said. "I spik English and I will understand."

"You will see," she went on, leaning heavily against my arm as we walked, "I will get you hot. You will have a big one."

In her bedroom, naked, she seemed even smaller, like a little nubile girl, and I reached out to her, and we hugged close and did nothing for a few minutes.

Then Sophy broke it off and went and sat up on the bed; like some bourgeois lady instructing her maid, she gave me the ground rules for our sexual encounter:

No kissing.

Man on the top because I looked so large.

She eats me but I must not eat her pussy.

No love bites.

Positively no more talking.

I was not to touch her clitoris.

"Half an hour either way," she said, "for $25."

"How much would you charge just to take a shower with me, Sophy?

"Now or later?"

"Only," I declared. "A shower and maybe another little hug."

Sophy cursed me. I must surely be a big sissy. She had such lust for me. Desire. Couldn't I tell?

"Don't you like?" She was pointing with a finger between her legs, and wiggling: *"Baby ooo,"* went Sophy.

Words like that.

She pointed again and with a little pout said, "I don't like this but this is the way it must be done. As if we were making a baby together."

Again I began to demur, but thought better of it, gave her another fifty-*cordoba* tip, and started to dress and leave.

Sophy no longer pretended she was angry. I had paid for her time, and she knew it. She might have liked more money; her life was costly to her and she was fearful.

As I went toward the door, she said, "I hate you and all your countrymen for what you have done to me and all my people . . . with these Somozas."

She hit the *z* hard, crudely, and glided off into a dull glazed look of reproachful silence again.

"Sophy," I told her: "You are a very clever woman *sin dudas* so I am sorry . . ."

"You I don't really hate," she went on. "But I feel sorry for you and I don't like you anymore because you don't want to make love."

"And neither do you," I reminded her.

"Who don't want to?" She seemed irate: *"What you say?"*

"You want the money," I explained.

"You, too," she said, and she sat back and folded her hands on her lap and mimicked me.

She looked very pretty, just like a little airport souvenir stand doll. Sophy said, "I hate my fucking country . . . and all these stinking cunts make me sick!'

"Suerte, Sophy."

"You, too," she replied, a little blankly.

The last I saw of Sophy, as I closed the door quietly, she sat naked with her knees up in the air, in bed, and brought a finger toward her vagina to give herself such pleasure as she would no longer allow any other living creature to give to her, if, indeed, she ever had.

It was dark outside on the street, though only just a little after six P.M. The National Guardsman on the corner pointed his grease gun at me and demanded to see my ID.

He was an old man, one of the auxiliaries who had been called up to replace the commandos and black berets fighting in Masaya and León.

When I showed him my credentials, he let me pass, but not before pointing a finger at me and giving me a reproach. *"Peligroso,"* he said. Dangerous. "There is nothing but whores around here, and *terroristas."*

"They're not the same," I said.

"Be careful for the bombs," the guard said as he gave me a little shove with the butt of his weapon to let me know I could go on my way. ●

A BRIEF INTERVIEW (LEÓN) (1981)

"Do you love women?"

"As a matter of public relations," the official replied. "It does seem better."

"And then?"

"Personally I prefer young men," he told me, "though it's best our public doesn't have that rubbed in their faces."

"Nor ours?"

"Exactly so." He is a very handsome, slim man with a small thin mustache and well-cut military clothes, a somewhat rakish air.

I said, "So many women in the States come back and say what a womanizer you are."

"I never argue with them."

"They're all so flattered."

"Women usually are. You know," he said, "I don't dislike women but I prefer some men. So I pretend I'm interested and Nicaragua makes new friends . . . and if I said men . . ."

"What then?" I asked.

"It's just not done openly in our society even now," he says. "I value my job and my commitments to the Revolution."

"*Claro.*"

"What about you?" he asks, with a squint.

"I really like women."

"You say the same things I say sometimes. Just like me."

He turns about with military precision to talk to someone else. ●

LILLIAN (1982)

At receptions, or private house parties given by Managua's arty set, Lillian was always showing up like something left unsaid from a prior evening; a meager slim dark woman with a brooding look. She always wore high-fashion clothing from Milan and Paris, was not unattractive, except for being so thin she seemed almost skimpy. And because she limped a little on one of her skinny legs, as people do who had polio when they were little, it was hard not to notice her, even on a dance floor full of moving bodies. Lillian's narrow form seemed to syncopate among the shadows of the other dancers.

She was from one of the well-off families, obviously, and her friends were all Sandies. In fact, I learned she had a small honorific position with one of the ministries. She never was with anybody, man or woman, in what seemed to be an attached sort of way. Always just seemed to be hanging about the edges of a conversation or a dinner party, a reminder, a reproach, this woman who bit on the inside of her mouth, was somewhat pained-looking and forbearing, as though engaging in sociability were some official function she would otherwise have avoided. My friends all said, "That's one you'll never get to know. Nobody ever has."

Whenever we were introduced, Lillian did seem rather distracted. I could never even make eye contact with her, and once, when I complimented her on a particularly fetching black sheath she wore with her shoulders bare to a performance at the National Theatre, she turned away from me before the words were out of my mouth, as though I'd offered to give her *cordobas* for dollars, or said something embarrassing, or perhaps obscene.

The trouble was I found myself looking for her whenever I came to a gathering, as though the evening would have been so much less official for me without this shy but elegant person making her appearance. If she was there, I would find myself gazing at her unproductively, and when she was not I always felt the loss was somehow due to my lack. Other arty friends started teasing me: Was I in love with Lillian? They thought it really very funny. But I wasn't even one bit in love. It was more like the itch of curiosity besetting my eyeballs. I couldn't rid myself of the sensation of locating her in any room I entered.

I really knew very little about Lillian and asked a lot of questions of others, but never got answers. People said they really didn't know much themselves, and besides it was a private matter. Managua's intelligentsia love secrets; in that world of cozy depravities, secrets are a form of privilege almost equal to having power or wealth.

At one July 19th victory celebration, I was told that Lillian's last name was Lara, she was distinctly related to a famous politician from the epoch of the Central American Republic, that she was having a party at her home in Colonia Dembach later in the evening, and I had her special invitation to come.

The person who told me was a writer for *Sábado,* the weekend literary supplement of the Party paper. I had work to do that evening, and by the time I got to Lillian's front gate, most of the official cars and bodyguards had left. An old servant woman in black led me out to the patio where Lillian sat like an exclamation point among her few remaining guests.

"Here comes a man wearing sandals," said the crone, announcing me. "*Ahi viene sandalista!*" Some people obliged her with a laugh, as was the custom.

There was a bar and a bowl of rum punch. I went over to Lillian and thanked her for the invitation.

"Ah yes," she said, casting her eyes down, "I had heard you've been asking questions about me."

"It's hard not to notice you," I said.

"Why?" She glanced up, genuinely surprised.

"You seem so different from the others," I said.

"Perhaps that's because I was raised in this place, and in convents," Lillian added. She faced out toward the darkness contained by high brick walls. Bits of broken glass on the walls glittered down on her patio. There were bright patches of tropical blossoms the color of blood when it is first exposed to air.

"My family has always been prominent in Nicaraguan affairs," she added with a smirk I interpreted as seductiveness.

I asked her if there had also been a certain involvement in "affairs inter-American."

"Catch as catch can," she replied, with a giggle which did not cover her gloominess for more than an instant, and left me feeling just as gloomy as she generally looked.

Lillian then told me to get myself something to drink, anything I liked; she even had scotch from a conference in Jamaica. I went over to the bar, and a moment later, she joined me.

"Did anybody tell you how I killed my father?" she asked.

Startled by her question, I dropped my glass on the table so that the ice rolled about like dice.

"I am sorry to hear that," I said at last, when I'd recuperated.

"It was most definitely a political act," she said, "and I have never been sorry. He was Somoza's pro-consul in Salvador. I was in the raiding party."

"You must have hated him very much," I said.

She glanced down again and her very bright lips trembled a moment: "The truth is I felt rather sorry for him, but it had to be done, to set an example."

She walked away, back to her company. The rest of the evening she kept to herself, and I kept my distance, suddenly rather fearful of what she might divulge about herself next, but when it was time to leave I went over to thank her for her hospitality.

"I think you are no longer curious about me," Lillian said, smiling faintly.

"Never more than was apropos," I said.

"For an enemy of humankind," she said. "You have nice long legs."

And when I hesitated, she added: "Now you say to me, 'Likewise, I'm sure.'"

"Likewise," I started to say, and remembered her meager lameness and said no more.

I said nothing more. There was really nothing I could tell her.

Some days later a friend mentioned that Lillian Etcheverria Lara, as he called her, was getting married pretty soon to my journalist friend from *Sábado* because she felt her biological clock ticking away and wished a baby. Such gossip — like secrets — are also among the privileges bestowed in a nation the size of Nicaragua on anybody with friends among the leading families, Conservative, Liberal, or Sandinista. Sooner or later one gets to know the name of every married woman's lover, and the time of their cycles. It's really all one big unhappy Nicaraguan family of sorts.

So I asked my friend if it was true that Lillian had killed her own father.

"Another woman did," he said, "of her own class; this Lillian is just flighty, I think, and unfriendly to Americans. But it's now one of the things women from her class are all saying of themselves."

Later, I wrote Lillian a note: "Congratulations on your marriage to my friend Salazar. He is a man of intelligence. But perhaps you have not heard so I will tell you: When my wife and I were making a baby we were told man on top or from behind was apt to be the most productive from a baby-making point of view . . . though willy-nilly is always pleasurable . . . here or in Wiwili."

A day or so later a special messenger came to my door with an envelope marked "diplomatic traffic."

I opened the envelope and there were Polaroid photos of Lillian with certain well-known members of her set going through the various baby-making positions, and some I had not even thought to mention.

I thought they were all singularly without eroticism, like the postures of the old primary school rhythmic gymnastics classes during the former regime.

There were almost as many as in a deck of cards, and all in sallow color, a little over-exposed, one ought to say.

On the back Lillian, or someone, scribbled a paraphrase of a line from an infamous poem by the party-line poet Gioconda Belli: "The special semen full of letters that fertilizes me is the work of many hands."

I wanted to write back and tell her I thought it was a lot better to fuck guys galore than kill your own father, though, as far as I was concerned, there were many worse sins than patricide, judging from my own experience. For example, saying you had done so to create a stir, an effect. A scandal—that was worse.

I never got a chance to say any of this to Lillian to her face because she was murdered in the north, only a few weeks later, in a Contra raid on one of the new *haciendas* where she and her husband from *Sábado* had gone to collect interviews for a book about the new Nicaraguan women and the revolution. ●

DINNER OUT (1981)

The Cuevas are giving dinner to their close friends and neighbors, the Vascos, at Tiscapa, in the restaurant with colored lights rimming the crater.

A lot of important people are eating nearby. Julio Cuevas makes a joke. "With prices like this one would have to be in the government."

A shot in the night, and Julio dives beneath the table, upsetting his wife's cream pudding on Juan Vasco's lap.

"That's what comes from having a guilty conscience," Marisa says.

Julio apologizes profusely. There's a crescent moon and he feels his forehead burning.

He says, "In Managua these days there is no such thing as an innocent statement."

"Surely." Friend Juan's seat is all wet. He spoons his pudding off his lap onto a plate. The Deputy Minister passes his table and slaps him on the shoulder. "Just remember. We need people like you to stay on."

Juan has almost slid off his seat.

"You flatter my friend," Julio declares.

"I would flatter you too if you would let me," the Minister says.

He bows toward the ladies, who take it as a cue to leave for the Ladies.

Julio says to Juan, "You must allow me to take the accounting." He signals the waiter.

"Enjoy your evening," the Minister says. "Be prudent." One two three four five six shots explode beyond the army barracks.

From under his table Cuevas says, "Much obliged. Thank you very much. Of course. Much obliged."●

IN WHAT THEY USED TO CALL VIETNAM (1983)

The Bishop of Rome comes to Managua, says mass before tens of thousands, including quite a number of Party hecklers. You recall that. It was a set-up job. John was on one of his tours, had a number of other Central American gigs scheduled, and not a lot of time. In his cavalcade were no red and black banners on display, no pilgrimages scheduled to the tomb of Fonseca, the birthplace of Sandino in Niquinhomo. As far as His Holiness is concerned, there's been only one martyr truly worthy of the Nicaraguan masses. He chats it up with the Chief of State, sees the bishops, reproaches some of the local clergy, and offers himself as host to the gullible faithful.

Sylvio Blanco attends the service. He's supposed to put the Pope on notice about the People's historic victory, but he really doesn't wish to seem rude, like some of the others. Sylvio is a member of the government textile union, but also a Catholic, in decent standing with his priest, and the Church. He has two different girlfriends and children by each one. He went to both baptisms. Sylvio knows the world he lives in is dangerous. His father lost his legs on the Granada Railroad. No point in taking unnecessary chances when you have no money in the bank. His father rolled around on a board with roller skates near the National Cathedral until he was run over by a jeep, and the army gave the family fifty dollars, which was a lot of money in those days for a legless beggar. Sylvio likes the Bishop because "he's an Indian with eggs," but he knows his own main chance is with the New Church.

After the service he goes to visit his mother in Vietnam where he grew up, only "they don't call it that anymore." He has a chocolate bar for her kids, and some Greek macaroni which she and his younger brothers and sisters will be glad to have.

His mother has boiled water for coffee. She even has milk. She makes him sit at the table. She's a religious woman but she never goes to church anymore. "I have my own religion in my heart," she says. "The spirits move me."

Sylvio hates all that superstition and he knows his mother will ask about his women, and the children, so in order to keep her mouth shut he begins about the Pope, so splendid and arrogant and blond in his white robes.

"Why did they heckle the Holy Father?" she asks her son.

"Because," he says, "we are the Children of God . . . even the people of this *barrio*."

She asks, "What do the bishops say about all this?"

"They say what bishops always say about respect," he answers her.

She scalds some milk and spoons out the costly Nicacafé powder into a cup, adds the milk and a little boiling water, even has some black sugar in a bowl for her son.

"Sylvio Humberto," she says, as he busies himself, "do you really think this Pope hates our Revolution?"

He explains to his mother that for people of our class it's really not so important to know what the Pope likes or dislikes. He's just another *cacique,* and they must learn to make their choices between these old-time *caciques* and the new.

He says, "This Pope is Polish. He comes for a visit but he goes back to Rome. A few hours preaching is hardly our lifetimes here."

"He has visited Nicaragua," she says with finality. She helps herself to a little coffee. "He took this trip here in a plane; and when you come to see us — and we are not so far away — you only stay a few hours."

"But I am always coming back," Sylvio reminds her.

She sips at her coffee, and peers at the rutted wooden table.

"Did Danilo Ortega ask the Pope to return?"

"How should I know that?" Sylvio shrugs. "They are both such important people."

"If John Paul wasn't invited back," she says, "how could he return?"

"Maybe so. So what?"

"If you ask me," she says, "this Pope is not just another Reagan."

"Nobody says he is," Sylvio protests, "but he is also not God. He's a man like all the rest of those who support the other side — and he uses the privy just like you and me."

"And does he read *Novedades* in there and later *Barricada,* just like you used to do, when others badly needed to heed the calls of nature?"

"Probably." Sylvio smiles at his mother's teasing. She's always trying to draw him back to that time when he was still her son, living at home, helping out.

He says, "The Church in Rome is wealthy. His Holiness doesn't need to use his reading materials as we do even now."

"Just the same," she says, "His Holiness came to visit Nicaragua and that never happened in all the years your father was alive — even the years when Tacho's father was alive."

"True," he says, "surely . . . and what do you make of that?"

"To me," she explains with her hand on her breast, "it must mean only one thing. These boys in the government must be very smart and even more, they have powers. Real powers."

"It's all sorcery," she adds. "Chango, plainly. They must be true wizards to bring this pope here in his white robes, and they so young. The man with the withered arm,

Danilo's brother, he could do the double talk just like your father."

"Plainly he is not afraid of his Holiness," adds Sylvio.

"Just as I thought," his mother says. "They are spirits."●

THE HOUSE WATCHER (1981)

For many years after the fall of Managua the Julio Blancos refused to live in their city house in the colonia. They stayed in the country on the farm and commuted when they had business in town. The city house was left vacant, shuttered, except for one brief period when it served as the temporary embassy for a Vietnamese diplomatic delegation. Julio Blanco used to say, "I walked in and there were the cooks sleeping in my father and mother's bed."

He was quite old and frail and he still had a little wealth, though very little desire except to be left alone to finish out his life in comfort on the soil of the fatherland. "Julio," his wife Xilma told guests, "hates the Revolution almost as much as he hated old Somoza's people."

Julio had his reasons. He'd not yet been robbed, but his son and daughter were both in military service and every servant they employed was an SDN from one of the Block committees whose job it was—he believed—to spy on them. So he released all his retainers and brought a cousin from the country whom he presumed would surely be trustworthy. Her name was Miranda and she was most certainly as dependable as an old watch in the service of the Party. Then Julio decided he would leave the splendid isolation of his country place and go to Managua. There, at least, he would have the opportunity to talk to foreigners.

The Blancos arrived in Managua on a day in Little Summer when the air was glittery with thousands of little volcanic cinders. Their taxi made its way through the battered streets to drop Julio and Doña Xilma and the dubiously faithful Miranda at the wrought-iron gates of "Pretty Vista." The walls were blanketed with bougainvilleas. There was wash fluttering on the lines they could see behind the garden wall. How desolate and sad their grand old place looked, a sickly and anemic shade of Naples yellow, with chocolate brown trim. Down their hill was the battered skull of the old Grand Hotel, a haunt of Julio's youth, and Lillian Snuya's Café Cocorico, long since shattered. The Gypsy Brothel, the English Club, the Ying-Yang Disco were all in the vicinity, and long since destroyed by earthquake or war, or shuttered down. Their own street, oddly, was decrepit, ill-kempt, but intact. "In Miami," Julio remarked, "we would not be strangers to anybody with a place such as this."

"You don't want to go to Miami," his wife told him. "You don't want to go anywhere except straight to bed." She opened the gate with her key and the trio approached the old battered wooden door.

A neighbor, meanwhile, appeared in the entryway to their left and neither Julio nor his wife recognized this person.

She was round and short, with skin so deep brown it seemed polished as though with ox blood. Her eyes were large and brown, she squinted occasionally, but her stare was frank, familiar. Her hair was black, straight, hacked short. She was barefooted. "I am Nelly Blandon," she introduced herself. "I was hardly more than a child when you left. But I have been watching your house for you all this time, I assure you, Don Julio, nothing has been touched."

"That's much appreciated," he said. "Do you live next door?"

"I sleep on your steps," she told him. "The people give me food. I was never your neighbor, *padrecito*. We lived in your back yard, and then you went away and locked the house and left us here."

She spoke with a flatness that some might confuse for bitterness. Julio and the women were startled by her words. They'd forgotten all about the family of squatters in the backyard. The lorry with their suitcases would not be arriving till after dark. Julio proposed that Nelly enter the house with them so he could make some kind of small appropriate settlement for her services.

"As you like," she said, as she climbed across the barrier wall and stood right beside them while Julio fished for his keys.

Nelly had a very powerful smell, he noticed, of woodsmoke and farm animals, but it was not too offensive to him.

He was offended, though, when Xilma extended her hand to the girl and introduced herself and Miranda. "We are certainly glad for your custodianship. To do all that without a gun," she announced.

"Guns are not necessary at this historical moment," Nelly observed. "Besides, my brother drives a Jeep for the Ministry of the Interior."

The door swung open on an atmosphere crystalline with dust and gloom. Nothing had changed except by gaining a sort of fur on every surface from all the years of vacancy.

The air was heavy and acrid; they glided along the terrazzo through the foyer and principal rooms toward the glass doors and patio beyond. All the furniture was sheeted and stained with mold.

In the patio the coffee bushes looked skimpy, berryless. Despite all these changes of atmosphere and desuetude, Julio thought the place was very much as he had left it; he believed he had Nelly to thank for that. If he'd once dropped some keys on one of the chairs, he believed they would still be there now, when he lifted up a sheet to look for them.

They were all standing in the sunroom, among the empty birdcages, when Doña Xilma recommended that they take seats and chat a bit. There was coffee in their travelling thermos and Miranda would find cups in the chiffonier and serve all of them.

Doña Xilma cringed a little when Nelly pulled away the sheet covering the Shlumberger loveseat from Miami and sat down on it, first with the bottoms of her thighs and then her bare bottom. "Make yourself at home please," Julio was saying. Outside a very loud demonstration of young Sandinistas was passing by, chanting "They Shall Not Pass" and other slogans.

Above the uproar Nelly said, "It's so different now than the way things used to be. People couldn't even walk on the streets . . . the Guard. For girls like me . . ."

"They were never so bad for us," Julio had to admit.

"I understand," she smiled at him benignly.

"Of course we all hated Somoza," Doña Xilma added. "Always."

Miranda entered the room with tiny white cups on a tray. *"Pues,"* said Nelly. "This is surely better than the stuff we are now forced to drink."

"A little better," Julio winked at her.

"We could give you some," Xilma said.

"It doesn't matter," Nelly shrugged. "We are used to these things. Ask your son."

"Do you know the boy?" Don Julio asked eagerly.

"He's not for people like me," said Nelly. "He's friends with Chamorros and top Party people — Sandinistas," she added.

Doña Xilma said, "I didn't know our sort were Sandinistas."

"Almost all are." Nelly said, "That's one thing that hasn't changed."

"Indeed," said Miranda. She began to pass out cups.

After coffee and chitchat, the two women of Don Julio Blanco began to remove all the sheets. They made a large bundle which they carried out into the patio. Then they went upstairs to make beds. Don Julio found his old humidor in the little secretary in the library containing one quite fresh cigar. He asked Nelly if she knew where there were matches. She reached inside a pocket of her flimsy frock and found a .50-caliber cartridge devised to be a flint lighter.

Don Julio enjoyed fooling with the lighter. It reminded him of a souvenir of the Great War in Europe; he had personally witnessed the beginnings of that in 1938 in Biarritz, when he'd gone with his cousin Federico to cure a broken heart. Doña Xilma was, at that time, just a little girl cousin from the family branch in Jinotega. When he returned he was introduced to her at his cousin's place at Montelimar and they were engaged to be married. He wished he could explain those times to this young peasant girl seated opposite him, but she would not understand, even if she cared to try. He got up and went out through the open glass doors into the patio.

Despite its evident neglect, that too was very much as Julio remembered it—aside from one large dark stain on the flagstones running back toward the laundry. Don Julio was afraid to ask what that stain might be. He kept staring at it, hoping Nelly would read his mind and tell him what it was. But she was pulling dead dry berries off one of the bushes. "If they wither on the vine," she pointed out, "nothing can take their places."

"It's all right," Don Julio told her. "What do I see here?" He pointed at the stain.

"I'm afraid it's nothing very much; there were militia stationed here and they killed a goat."

"Puta!" Don Julio swore. He was finding it hard to believe what he was being told.

"Are you telling me there were no executions?" he demanded.

"Oh, yes, there were a few, but not here," Nelly added. "Elsewhere."

The women returned a few moments later and invited Don Julio up to see his bedroom, which had been freshened and made ready for him. He, in turn, suggested that

Nelly come along, as he was not finished talking to her.

They went up the stairs one at a time, with old Don Julio, frail even for his years, taking up the middle with one hand on the stair rail. Strong afternoon light from a clear window at the turning in the stairs illuminated them harshly, as though they were pilgrims ascending a shrine.

Upstairs a breeze stirred the graying haze of the formerly white organdy curtains. In Don Julio's bedroom, panelled with orangy-brown lignum vitae, a strong musty smell, almost like snuff or camphor that has moldered a little, engorged their nostrils. The three women led Don Julio to the chaise at the foot of his bed and asked him to stretch out for a while.

The old man seemed suspicious of the attentions he was receiving, and once more turned to Nelly: "Tell me, Little Snapdragon, why an old man like me should receive such a welcome here?"

She smiled with knowing condescension and bent down in front of him to remove his boots. Don Julio thought he could see her small bulbous bosoms emerge from the front of her dress. He thought she was so much like Dora, his India, so soft with her favors, so fierce in his arms. *"Padrecito,"* she said, "in our eyes you will always be a father no matter what you may have done."

"But I did nothing — *never*," he protested.

"Exactly," Miranda said, "and that is why your children fight for the Marxists."

Nelly came closer to him and caressed his stockinged feet, as though articles of papal reverence. "Now," she said, "before this day is over you must acknowledge me to the Law, or the Church, it does not matter. For propriety's sake . . ."

The other two women hissed, as though to defy her or acknowledge her, he didn't know, and he was more flattered than astonished by this woman-child's demand.

"What should I acknowledge you as?" Don Julio inquired. "How shall I put it?"

"That I am your daughter, as my mother was almost assuredly your back-yard wife."

"That?" He felt a warmth spreading through him. Once it was called to his attention there was surely no doubting she was Dora's child. He'd simply not chosen to look at her that way. All these years, he thought, a lifetime since our moments together, her lifetime.

Don Julio was not an unreasonable person and, if it was up to him alone, he would have gladly stretched his arms out to Nelly even now as the child of his back-yard wife, but he had his own children to consider and the feelings of his legitimate wife. For that reason he hesitated. He even tried to appease: "We should consult a priest. There must be ceremonies . . . forms . . . the right way."

"Momma was a Protestant," Nelly reminded. "She was Moravian; you, as I recall, were a Freemason."

"It doesn't matter," he explained. "It would just be a ritual for you and me."

The other women were losing their patience. "Why not give her the house and the farm, too?" Doña Xilma asked harshly. "Anything to make up for your terrible lusts."

He stared at her as though looks could maim, if not kill, but said to Nelly: "If you insist, child, I will acknowledge you this very day. Anyway you please."

"With a kiss in front of all the neighbors should suffice for this moment," she declared. "The rest are bourgeois legalisms. Come, Papa," she added, "let me take you by the hands out into the open air of the street."

A strange procession clanged upon the iron gates of "Pretty Vista" and went out into the bright air of the *barrio* street that afternoon, just as a Toyota lorry was pulling up, crammed high with parcels and valises.

Leading the procession was old Don Julio himself, dressed in well-pressed dark trousers and his immaculate white linen jacket; on his arm was this dark cinder of a streetgirl, his bastard Nelly. Don Julio's wife and niece followed at some five paces. The day had changed. Under a humid sky the color of semen they entered the street. When they stood together on the paving stones, Don Julio called out to all the people in the block to please stick their heads out their windows, come to their doorways. His neighbor Amanda Reyes saw what was happening and told her sister, "First he spits in the bowl and then he offers us the scraps."

Don Julio raised Nelly's arm high in the air and said, "People of my *barrio*, friends and neighbors: I wish to make it known to one and all that Nelly here, whom you all know as the girl Nelly of the Back Yard, is my daughter, and the child of love."

"And I am nobody's bastard?" she added.

"There was love between your mother and me," Don Julio said, "and that gives you legitimacy."

"Did you all hear?" Nelly announced with her hands up to her face like a megaphone.

There was a spattering of applause from open windows and some of the children came forward to view this odd family. Then somebody turned on a gramophone and the Red Army chorus of the Soviet Union sang a march. People from nearby *esquinas* began to appear and loiter. Don Julio, meanwhile, continued to hold Nelly's hand aloft, as though she were a victorious prizefighter.

The local block committee, meanwhile, was consulting the Police as the crowd in front of Don Julio's place grew larger.

"Many years ago on my farm," he was saying, in a soft furry voice, "I met a woman in the fields and she was very beautiful to me, and without my wife's knowledge I installed her in the laundry shacks in my backyard. Her name was Dora and Nelly was her daughter. And she was very beautiful to me."

"And he was never anything but an old billy goat," Miranda stepped forward to announce.

Don Julio replied: "Even billy goats must eat or they starve."

The cars arrived only a few minutes later to take Don Julio into custody for creating a disturbance. He was not treated harshly in the place where he was sent, but when he was released some days later it was clear that he might be dying very soon, and Doña Xilma sent Miranda and Nelly to the farm to begin preparations for the old hidalgo's burial. ●

DON'T TURN RIGHT (1984)

Prudhomme got married on the beach at San Juan Del Sur. Jenny Margulies of *Aperture* took photos and the ceremony was performed by a Maryknoll from Sandino City.

He stood with his bride beneath a *rojonegro* scarf held aloft by two of his friends in the press while the Father intoned the words as revised by the liberation church. Their wedding rings were of bronze, meltdowns of shell casings. When Prudhomme bent to kiss his bride, she leaned against his arms in a revolutionary *abrazo*.

It was Cara's idea. She was still Catholic, sufficiently so, she did not wish an abortion, and she was very pregnant. Their divorce would be forthcoming upon the birth of the child. Prudhomme had given her over 30,000 francs.

The six of us took lunch afterwards at the terraced seafood restaurant above the fishing port. Down below the Russians were building a base for their Pacific tuna fleet. Some said it might also service submarines.

Prudhomme had gotten shrimps and sole from a friend on one of the boats. We had a tomato salad, bread, Salva Vida beer from Honduras, and local brandy, a festive repast for Nicaragua Libre.

Cara seemed very uncomfortable in her beige tunic. Her belly could not be contained. She looked pale and grim and then with a drink, she was giggly, gabby.

"Now I know how the Cubans feel," she said. "At any moment the Yankees could wipe them out and yet they go on celebrating weddings, having babies . . ."

"When they can," Prudhomme added.

He sat straight in his chair and poured out another round of beers. He spoke softly, so as not to be overheard by the waiters.

"I was in Cuba in '62 after Krushchev withdrew his missiles. Yes, they were there, Cara darling," he added, "and

Fidel was very angry with the Soviets for backing down. The rest of us were celebrating that we would live to tell the tale, but in front of a huge crowd Fidel made fun of Krushchev. He called him 'fag,' 'Nikita Mariquito,' 'Nicky the Sissy.' Not much fun in that fellow I can testify."

He reached for his bride's hand and kissed it, like a courtier, but she remained stiff and distant, drew back from him as though reproachful, leaving the imprint of his kiss upon the air. "Fidel maybe wished a Third World War," Prudhomme went on. "Didn't matter if Cuba was annihilated."

"That's stupid," Cara said. "It can't be true."

"I heard it with my own ears," Prudhomme said. He wet his silky brown mustache with his tongue. He raised his glass as though to make a toast: "You should leave the country with me . . . as my wife . . . on my passport."

"I wish our child to be Nicaraguan," Cara insisted.

"If he lives so long," Prudhomme said.

"It won't be our fault if he doesn't," said Sanchez, Cara's colleague in the Ministry.

Prudhomme sneered at the fellow. We fell silent again.

Jenny and the Maryknoll were going off to Rivas to visit a new day care center. Though we weren't asked to, the rest of us got out of our chairs when they departed, and then sat down again. Prudhomme's bronze ring caught a glimmer of sunlight when he ran his fingers through his hair. He said, "When it's safe you can come back. A child needs adequate medical care, a sheltered environment, nourishment."

"I intend to nurse my baby," Cara said.

"I'm sure," Prudhomme said, "if your milk comes, as it must, and the new midwives are very skilled. That goes without saying," he added "it must be so. But I should like to keep an eye on you both."

"Then you should stay," she spoke hoarsely. "The rest is scared talk."

"I am scared sometimes," he said.

"You are not having this baby," she replied.

In Spanish I tried to recite the old proverb to Cara by the learned Golden Age rabbi that "a thing is no less true because a Jew has said it."

"We need Demerol, not proverbs," Cara said, "but we will manage. This is not the first baby born in Nicaragua — with Cuban forceps. I am assured the birth will be uncomplicated."

"Let us presume," Prudhomme said.

A pouting face needs no explanations, but I realized his pout was an expression of trying to care. "Words sometimes hurt," he mused.

"Not like bullets," Sanchez said.

He stood up and moved out of the sun beneath an umbrella. "We should be going back soon."

"What? And miss our honeymoon?" Prudhomme laughed harshly.

"You had your fun with me already," Cara said.

"Her belly does not belie that fact," Prudhomme observed.

Cara said, "I hate puns. My English never catches on."

"Never mind," Prudhomme said.

"May I kiss the bride?" I said, as I bent and touched her warm yeasty face with my lips.

Cara, who did not love me, threw up her hands: "Maybe I should cry rape."

"Maybe I should cry too," I said.

Then I sat down again and started to tell them about my friend Marco's daughter. She was a diabetic. They took her to the hospital in a coma and gave her glucose because there was no insulin, and she died the same night. "It's nobody's fault," Prudhomme shrugged. "Paramedics often lack training."

"These things happen because of the embargo," Cara said. "You Americans kill in many ways."

To argue against what was undeniable was foolish. Prudhomme, nevertheless, could not let the matter rest. "It's alright dying so long as you can blame it on the *gringos?*" he demanded.

Cara stood up: "I wish to go back to work now."

I paid our bill, and Sanchez suggested I add some of my cigarettes to the tip.

We walked down the hill toward our car, Cara protruding against the humid air like an overloaded barge.

Against a backdrop of calm gray cove water, she intruded on my peripheral vision with belly and thigh.

As Prudhomme was unlocking the door, our waiter came running down the hill. He was calling out to us: "*Compañeros.*"

"Now we see how a generous tip can affect solidarity," Prudhomme joked.

The man was dark and narrow faced. He had greasy black hair. He was rasping to catch his breath. If the other *compañeros* have now gone off elsewhere, perhaps the remaining *compañeros* would have room to drive him to Managua. He wished to visit his wife and child in a *colonia* near the Laguna in Managua. It had been three weeks since he had seen them.

Prudhomme was annoyed at the intrusion, but seemed willing to oblige, perhaps to please his new bride. Cara, on the other hand, flew off the handle.

"When are we going to stop being a nation of beggars?" she demanded.

She turned on the little man. "These people have important things to talk about. They may not wish you to overhear them."

"I yam discretion," the fellow announced in English.

"What is the harm?" Prudhomme asked. He was holding open the door so Cara could get inside. She stayed in place.

"I don't want to ride with this person," she said. "He could be anybody."

"I support the government of the FSLN," the man protested. "I am a waiter. Ask anybody."

Prudhomme let himself in and turned over the motor
and clicked on the air conditioning.

"I'm afraid I cannot help you," he told the fellow.

He felt the air with his open palm and, when it seemed
cool enough, motioned for Cara and Sanchez and me to
come inside.

As we drove off, kicking up the dirt, I saw the man in
his plain white shirt and dark trousers engulfed in a cloud
of our dust.

"He's a new type," said Sanchez. "Always testing the
Revolution, as though it meant *mozos* and *comandantes* all
sleep in the same beds, and that is popular power."

"It's a joke," Prudhomme said. "But perhaps he was desperate to see his family."

Sanchez said, "There are buses."

"The truth is little worms like that don't even believe in
popular power," Cara added. "They just want a little more
from the System and they are envious."

"With some reason," I said.

"There are ways to advance," Sanchez said. "Let him try
to write his own name first. We want people to move up
the ladder."

"Meantime take the bus," Prudhomme said.

He accelerated and drove us out along the wet flatlands
toward the highway.

"I certainly didn't wish to add to your discomfort,"
Prudhomme said, as though their words had reproached
him.

"My discomfort has not a thing to do with it," Cara told
him.

We bumped our way across a narrow-gauge railway
track.

"Somewhere along here was where Pastora tried to
break through in July '79," I said.

"It must be over that way," Prudhomme said, as he turned the car toward a narrow rutted land between fields.

"Don't turn right," Cara said.

We straightened out again and eventually turned left onto the *carretera* south heading north for Managua.●

NEAR THE CAMPO DE MARZO (1979)

In September 1979, the FSLN started reburying its dead. Each of the fallen martyrs was given a special funeral by surviving comrades and interred at the places where he or she had died, in most cases. It was a very hot and sunny month, humid at times, as though the air of the country-side, after so much violence and anarchic celebration, was putrefying.

Prudhomme told me he and Cara slept naked, covered only by the night. He sometimes said he had bad dreams. It was better to be with Cara than sleeping alone.

Inside so much mosquito netting the air was humid, as when they cure tobacco leaves. Light from the corner traffic intersection tinged their bodies green and red. Cara said Prudhomme looked "odious but sexy."

"Can that be?" He peered at her solid hip.

She moved closer to him and he felt her body was as damp as his own. A faint smell of almonds.

It was very late. Cara had to report early to her job. Prudhomme said he would be going off later in the morning by car to Jinotega to watch the army search for another band of armed stragglers from the Guardia. Though the victory and capitulation had been entire, the Party press was already speaking of counterrevolution.

"One war ends and another begins," he said.

"Everything has changed. Nothing is like it was," she reminded him, as though misunderstanding.

"Before—?" he asked, moving even closer to her so that their bodies seemed to adhere.

"I never think of dying until afterwards," Cara said. "Before I try not to think of anything."

"And sometimes you think of dying?"

"Sometimes," she said. "But not now."

She caressed his face and kissed his shoulder.

"Carajo! What's that?" He'd started to tremble. Volleys of rifle fire shattered the silence. Near the old army base they spattered and subsided and spattered twice more.

"What's going on?" he asked.

"Stay away from the windows," Cara said. "It's dangerous."

He told me some months later they overlooked the barracks, but not the parade grounds, illuminated by glaring sodium lights. He backed away and ducked beneath their net. Their bodies touched. Again there were volleys, three in a row, about a minute apart, spaced deliberately, he thought.

It was rather an odd time of the night for target firing.

"The soldiers are probably drunk, and shooting off their weapons. A waste of ammunition. But what can one do? Some are so young."

Prudhomme thought yes and no. He thought he could detect design. These didn't sound like rowdy displays.

There was another *baroom* and then, moments later, isolated pistol shots.

"I hope somebody tells them to cease," he said.

"Soon," Cara whispered. "I am sure of it."

There was a final volley five minutes later and then the night was very quiet and they dozed.

He woke early and went immediately to the windows. Two olive-painted panel trucks were parked opposite the high brick wall of the parade ground with their rear doors ajar. Some soldiers were toting large canvas sacks of mail, or tarpaulins, he couldn't be sure which, and stowing them in the trucks.

When he turned about Cara sat up in bed. She was smoking. Her hair was all scuzzied with sweat and she was smiling at him, though not necessarily in a pleasing way.

"Now the whole world will know," she said, "because of my journalist friend."

"You overestimate my influence," Prudhomme said, suddenly aware of what he'd heard and seen.

"They were all killers and rapists," Cara said. *"Lice!"*

She had tears in her eyes. "I couldn't sleep at all. My generation has known nothing but hate; last night that ended."

A truck revved its motor. He felt displeased with Cara for not telling him there would be firing squads last night. He'd heard rumors about Granada and other places, but believed the official explanation that a sad and battered country would not now resort to vengeance.

"I can't say I'm weeping," he told her. "I wish I could."

"Why?" she asked. "Why?" she repeated the question.

He shrugged at her. He couldn't explain such wishes to Cara. She would regard them as quirky at best.

"It's finished," she said. "It may not happen ever again. Isn't that better?"

"I don't know."

"The air smells of death," he added as a breeze lifted the curtains. "It smelled that way in June and July."

"You're mistaken," she said. "What you smell are diesel fumes."●

THE OLD WOMAN'S STORIES (1981)

"Anaya was a man from Rivas who went across the border into Guanacaste Province in Costa Rica to buy his wife a pair of pinking scissors, and when he came back he was stopped and arrested for being in possession of a weapon."

• • •

"The Greytown woman told the nephew of Cruz he didn't look much like a communist. He should wear eyeglasses."

• • •

"In my village of Masatepe I once saw with my own eyes Sandino on a horse. He looked better than any Christ, handsome and small, swarthy like an Indian. He asked me if I played with dolls. I was five years old."

• • •

"Don't believe the people who tell you everybody had it bad under Somoza. Some of the people in this government—their families didn't make their *tortas* out of the roadside dust."

• • •

"So many people have been murdered in Nicaragua, so many maimed and orphaned, so many in the family album of cadavers; I expect to pass on soon and it will be like a reunion for me. I have many more dead friends than friends alive, young as well as old, and all my sons were martyrs. It will be such a party with rum to drink and maybe even pork, and the first thing I know all these dead will ask me is 'who can we expect next?' " •

THE OLD MAN'S STORIES (1979)

"During the struggle a man was shot right in front of that cobbler's shop. He was carrying home a fish from the lake for his family, and nobody came for him for a day or more. People said it was the fish which stank so much."

• • •

"I once saw Tacho with Turner Shelton, the American ambassador. It was near Montelimar where he had his big estate. They were riding together, fine white horses, in the English manner. I thought that was very amusing because Tacho had a big rear end, and when he went up and down, so did it—boompadoomp. Like that. The American wore a bush jacket and a bush hat. He looked like he could have been in South Africa or Australia."

• • •

"There are still some very pricey whores in Nicaragua, despite the new laws. One I heard about from my cousin who is with the diplomatic service calls herself Nancy Reagan, and she has straw-colored hair, and when you take her she recites 'The Star Spangled Banner.' "

• • •

"We have the best beef in the world, but we sold it to the fast-food transnationals . . . and nobody knows to go into a store and ask for our coffee. Our long fibre cotton rivals Egypt's. We have hardwoods, and the sea on both sides of us is alive with fish and crustaceans.

"It's obvious to me why we still have to suffer so many privations. Sandino once said we are rich by providence and poor by design. Where the sea cow nibbles the mossy East Coast are we likely to find oil?

"The father of the present foreign minister, D'Escoto, used to own land there and it's said he knew there was oil, but he and the Americans had an understanding. They would build a refinery near Managua to process their oil at a profit to them, in return for which we would not look for our own supplies.

"Until recently that's the way such deals were always made in Nicaragua."●

THE GULF OF FONSECA (1981)

The hospital was low built of bright orange stucco; it looked somewhat like a motel without a neon vacancy sign jutting out. There was a narrow black cross made of hammered iron fastened to the front facade from which the red and black Sandinista flag, and the blue and white flag of the old Republic, jutted forth on poles.

Through a tangle of papers and bloody gauze, fly-blown remains dumped on the front lawn, Fonseca walked into the main entry and found the patients' registry and sought out his wife's room.

He was a tall slim man, and he wore a baseball cap advertising Purina Feeds and newly pressed khakis. Even that early in the morning the smell of rot and disinfectant stuffed his nostrils so that he was aware he might gag.

All the hospital staff dressed in gauzy green gowns. A soldier in dark green camouflage fatigues guarded the locked dispensary door with an AK.

Fonseca didn't have far to go. Tiana lay in a first-floor room behind a white gauze screen in bed with the infant. Behind another white gauze screen, which served as a room divider, another patient seemed to be suffering through the early stages of her labor in Spanglais: "OK . . . okey dokey . . . hola . . . guys please . . . *por favor!*"

He'd seen his baby girl yesterday, briefly, in the birthing room. Now he was struck once again by the perfect wonder of her form and face, her miniature intactness snuggling, in a light bunting, against Tiana's warm tan arm.

Mother and child seemed to be dozing. Fonseca didn't care to wake them. As he crossed the threshold, his wife sensed his presence. "*Mi amor?* Federico?"

He told her yes.

"Now we all look beautiful?"

"That's true," he said. "Beautiful . . . *okah.*"

He found a chair and sat beside her and reached for her other hand. She held it back. "They've asked me what we intend to name her."

"And what did you say?"

"I told them," she sighed softly, with her eyes closed, "we had no names picked out. We were waiting."

"To see, yes," he agreed.

The child breathed heavily, her face reddened. Tiana smoothed her forehead with the flat of her long finger. "I don't like Amador. I don't like Nora. None of the revolutionary names suit this baby."

"The Pochos chose Bianca," he reminded her, "they chose Bianca after Sandino's wife."

"It's all rock and roll with them," she giggled in English.

"Quiet." He put his finger to his lips, and then pulled it away again. "We could call her certainly after your mother or my father."

"Yes, won't that be nice?" She giggled again.

"Shush," He warned her.

"Yes." She closed her eyes as though to consider the question in all seriousness. "They say children with certain names will be having a definite edge in school and later life."

"Who knows if we'll stay that long," he reminded her, with a whisper. "Don't tell them anything. Tell them we will decide when we are all at home together and have been to the cemetery."

"Yes."

Federico knew he must go off to work. Promising to come back at the noon hour, he bent and kissed his wife's cool face and ran his fingers slowly through the mass of her rich dark hair.

"I will try to give her my milk today," she said, as he left. "It takes a while for the milk to come and with that person over there trying to squeeze out a MiG-21 it's a distraction. I could dry up. So I may ask them to take me into the hall, or the garden."

"It smells awful there," he said. "You should be careful how you put it. You don't wish to seem unnecessarily critical."

"I shall be like a schoolgirl," Tiana said.

Federico stayed a moment longer, silently, and then blew a kiss at his wife and beautiful new child and headed for the entry once more. As he went along the hall, he saw Seraño, his wife's doctor; the man was busy with charts, and nodded at him as though he were a stranger.

As Federico went toward the outer door the reek of rot and disinfectant again had him choking back a brief paroxysm of nausea.

A woman in black sat on the stoop selling tiny German silver and pewter effigies from Mexico. Federico was in a somewhat loving and playful mood, so he considered buying a pair of breasts with tiny nipples, the whole no larger than a holy medal, to give to Tiana when he saw her later.

"I also have the infant suckling," the old woman said.

"Just the breasts, *gracias,*" he said.

The day was beginning hot and slow, as though the air were a thick clear syrup poured across the earth, the climbing vines on walls and houses crystalline with bright garish colors.

Federico headed for the *carretera* and already the little boys were out everywhere, dodging his shadow, hawking chewing gum, black market razors, and newspapers. He bought *Nuevo Diario:* "CONTRAS EN MANAGUA".

Walking on, he read of a nest of armed counterrevolutionaries apprehended only the previous evening by forces of the Interior Ministry near the American school, a few esquinas to the south of where he now stood. The newspaper said this gang was calling itself "Miami Vice."

Federico needed coffee, and he wished he had time to stop somewhere.

A sound truck started down the street advertising the latest decrees on hoarding canned fish and beef. Neither items had been seen in Managua in quite some time. He must remember to clear his shelves at home of what they still retained from Cousin Flacco's visit while his wife remained in the hospital. He would store these Costa Rican delicacies in his father's old sailor chest from Corinto.

He came to his bus stop and waited, with his eyes diverted by cartoons of Tío Sam in a girl's dress pretending to be too shy and virginal to appear before all the gowned grown men at the World Court. Tío Sam stood in the entryway blushing, as though naked, with his legs crossed, his chin tucked down against his vest to subdue his pointy white beard. The caption read: "His first time, but who knows if the virgin is truly intact?"

Finally Federico's bus came along, with a tinny clattering of loose parts. He was the only person to climb aboard, and recognized his usual driver, Gato, who told him they would have to stop for water somewhere soon as the damned thing was overheating. Peering back into the coach when he took his seat, Federico observed the bus was nearly empty.

Federico said, "I don't wish to be late for my job."

"Have no fear," the driver told him. "No problem. There'll be self-defense drills all day. Nothing gets done in Managua today. It's the way."

They sped off.

When they arrived before the office of collections at the National Palace, all the staff were standing in an empty lot full of rubble across the way, armed with picks and shovels and a few weapons. He looked for his mates and found them in a mass toward the rear.

"How is Tiana?" his friend Vitas asked when he joined them. "And the baby?"

He allowed they were both doing fine.

His friend handed him a heavy pick.

"Today is for digging . . . bomb trenches and field latrines. We're the lucky chaps. The people from Claims will be going into the country."

"Going into the country" was a euphemism for work in the North, where it was quite dangerous. Federico was very familiar with the term. He said, "I was hoping to visit Tiana today at lunch."

"Just be patient," his friend said.

Soon they were marched off.

At lunch time he was so filthy and tired he bought a *torta* and a plastic bag of punch from a peddler and lay under an almond tree with his friends and dozed. Tiana would surely understand if he came after work. Her stepparents would be on hand if she needed anything.

He told Vitas, "You can't imagine how beautiful it is to have a child and a loving wife."

And he dozed ten minutes beyond lunch.

Sometime in the early afternoon, Federico was making up for lost time and raised his pick so high in the air above his head it fell, against his will, right across the top of his sneakered foot. The pain was so intense he passed out.

When he awoke he was in a dispensary and his foot throbbed as though it were made out of explosives. A kind *cumpa* said, "We have nothing here for the pain except aspirin and that will make you nauseous again. But someone has gone to fetch ice and a doctor."

"My wife is already in the hospital," he said.

"Anything serious friend?"

"A baby—our first." His eyes filmed with tears; the pain was distracting him.

"It's the way things get done in our time," she said. "You gain a child and maybe lose part of your foot."

He passed out again and did not wake until the operating room lights were glaring down against his eyes. He thought he could hear the sound a saw makes. There was no pain. In his drowse Federico thought he heard the surgeon say, "Our way to give a man a leg up in our society is to remove one of his feet."

"That's very funny," he said, laughing, but when he tried to pull himself up from the cot he was strapped down tight, and he started to shout: "Don't you dare! My child will need all of me!"

"Too bad for you, friend" the doctor said as he sawed through and something heavy fell onto the floor.

When he woke up it was because a fly was bothering his nose. Tiana stood over him in a dressing gown. Her stepmother held the baby close.

"*Mi amor?*"

"I'm a cripple?" he asked.

"A refugee," she said. "The government will be only too glad if we leave now."

"Poor Nicaragua," her stepmother said.

Tiana bent over and kissed his face many times. He felt a pinching at the bottom of his ankle, but nothing worse, when he tried to wiggle his toes.

"Poor Nicaragua," the woman said another time.

"The baby takes my milk," Tiana whispered. "She loves my milk—and we are calling her, with your permission, Gabriella."

He shrugged: "It's a beautiful name."

"We'll be happy elsewhere," she told him.

"Footloose," he muttered in English, a language Tiana still really didn't understand. ●

LOVING STRANGERS (1984)

In the middle of the night he heard a blabbering loud voice, a crying-out voice that tore him from sleep. He went to the window and peered down into the miasma of the darkened street.

Footsteps slapped the pavement. Metal jiggled, as though someone were getting ready to fire off a gun.

He looked directly below just as a dark figure streaked across his vision.

"Who is it? What are you doing?" Ismelda asked.

"It must be the Police again," Salvadore said. "Or the militia. *They* couldn't be so far south."

"I don't understand you." She was sitting up in the bed now, draped inside the bedclothes.

"The insurgents," he pointed out. "I thought it could be one of them."

"You mean the enemy?" Her voice carried with it a correction.

"The enemy." He repeated her word.

"Simeon," she added, softly, calling him by a love name, "Come back to bed."

Gunfire blasted.

"Simeon, back to bed," she said.

He turned away from the window in a crouch.

"It could be thieves," he shrugged at her softly.

"Come back to bed."

"He ran right in front of our door. He could be somebody we know."

"We don't know anybody anymore," she reminded him. "Come away. Come now."

He climbed in beside her and reached for her body. She allowed him to draw her close.

"Boy," she said, like a friend, "you have to watch yourself close all the time. This is not your fight." She stroked

they used their feet to push open an entrance and fired short heavy bursts with automatic weapons about the shacks.

I clung to my buttressed wall with my eyes closed and my ripped white banner jutting from me, hoping I would not be noticed. I clung to the wall as though a part of the architecture. Now I know that many of those soldiers who passed me in that alleyway were from an elite battalion and are probably dead, like so many leftist rebels I came to meet in those days. But it was my own life that drew me to that wall, like a supplicant, at that moment. I wondered what dying would be like and how taking a bullet might feel. Would I collapse? See black? Die?

I shook my head. My sweat was heavy. The soldiers had all moved on. They were shooting up shacks at the far end of the road. I thought it was safe to move on now, though my legs were trembling as I stepped.

Everywhere I stepped were clinking cartridge casings, and when I reached the end of the alleyway which opened onto a large sunny courtyard, my colleagues were waiting for me. My clothing was drenched.

"You almost got us killed," the woman said.

"I lack courage," I said.

"It wasn't that," she told me. "You weren't smart. It's safer getting behind the shooting."

I shrugged.

"I'm glad you're all right," my other colleague said. "Let's get out of here."

"Are there a lot of corpses?" I asked.

"Are you just asking," the woman said, "or do you really want to know?"

"Both and neither," I said.

She shrugged again and led the way around the other side of the church where some bodies were piled up like chunks of fruit in a huge open-face pie. They were probably all civilians. In my imagination, I saw my own body piled with all these others.

"Did this happen just now?" I asked, and shuddered.

"All day long," she said. "It's been a very bad day."

The air smelled of blood and soil. A guardsman stood to one side of all these with his rifle pointed downward as though he were working a pneumatic drill.

Noticing me, he said in Spanish *"no fotos!"*

"I was just looking," I said.

"Go away," he said. "These are the dead."

I rejoined my colleagues just as the shooting started again.

"We should get out of here," the woman said.

"I'm sorry," I told her. "I'm real sorry. I'm sorry."●

LOSING PARTS (1984)

I once saw a street fighter squeeze off numerous rounds with a Spanish automatic before he looked down and saw his barrel had dropped off. He was holding just the stock attached to the trigger. He threw the thing away and ran like hell.

On the day Prudhomme lost his right hand we'd gone to watch some maneuvers with the new Soviet tanks from Libya. There were about ten on display in a field outside Boaco. We left our car to inspect the merchandise and Prudhomme, as was his wont, put one hand on the fender of the tank to peer down underneath.

He started to scream like hell. He'd touched an exhaust manifold. The flesh stuck: the hand adhered.

If you told a child don't touch a hot stove and he continued to make the move you could slap the kid. How could you slap a veteran journalist? He couldn't get his hand away. I saw every move and didn't stop him until his face seemed to blank out all expression and his screaming numbed the searing heat.

I went to help him but he called out, "Don't."

Prudhomme was holding up his hand, glaring at the cooked flesh, and then he fainted. I held him back from falling, dropped him easily down onto the weedy ground.

His hand looked like blackened fish. It made me nauseous. By then others were with us. Prudhomme wept and pleaded with his pain. I asked for ice or butter or salve, but they only brought pink punch water. It was all the army had. I used it on his brow, and poured some cold water from my canteen over his hand.

Then I had some people help me load him with his pink-tinged face into the front seat of the car and we went off to the dispensary in Boaco.

It was a ten-mile drive and he was weeping, pleading with me with the pain again, while I pleaded with him not to touch it. Let it rest inside its soaking piece of rag.

When we got to the dispensary it was closed down and I figured it best to drive on to the big Catholic hospital in Managua, maybe twenty miles away. I got some ice and fresh cotton cloth and wrapped it around his hand.

"I am a dead man," he told me. "That fucking tank."

"Don't be silly," I said. "It's your hand."

"Fuck," he said, and fainted again.

In Managua I asked two soldiers in a jeep to guide us to the hospital. They drove ahead of us for a while and then disappeared.

In the hospital two nuns assured me I'd done the right thing. They carried Prudhomme away in a chair and told me to get some rest.

I went back to our hotel and took a shower and had a bite to eat. When I got back to the hospital some hours later Prudhomme was in the recovery room. He only had one hand above the covers. The left arm ended in a gauzy wrist.

He saw me looking. I couldn't lie about things.

"It's all right," he said. "I don't really mind. It was all my fault. There was nothing to save, I'm afraid. I am surely not some Hollywood shit. Ooo —."

The pain was coming on again. I told him "rest."

"I'm going back to France," he said, "for prosthesis. It's already been arranged."

I said I'd come back tomorrow.

"Yes you will do that," he said, "I know." His face was so pale. "I am such a stupid man. Really."

"It couldn't be helped," I lied.

"Like everything else in this country," he smiled. "It certainly could."

He closed his eyes. "Fucking tank."

I turned and left the room. I never saw Prudhomme again, but he did write me a letter once or twice, one of which appears hereafter as "Prudhomme's Story."●

PRUDHOMME'S STORY (1984)

I once met Che Guevara in Havana, it must have been 1960 or '61, but before the Bay of Pigs, as I recall.

It was at a reception at an embassy. This undoubted intellectual strode across the room like a warrior. He actually seemed to goose-step, big long heavy strides, such as none of us effete university types might take.

And when he arrived at his destination, he shook the ambassador's hand and made an about-face and strode back again.

I was very impressed. This was the way a man was supposed to behave. He had a bodyguard with a machine pistol, but when he went toward the buffet I followed.

Guevara must have heard my footsteps. He did another about-face.

"I wish only to shake the hand of the savant of guerrilla warfare," I said.

"You cannot shake the hand of a flea," Guevara told me.

He kept himself apart from people for as long as he stayed, and that wasn't very long. Suddenly, at a signal of his shoulder, he made another about-face, and so did his bodyguard, and the two left the room together.

Some months later he left Cuba forever.

They say when Eden Pastora first broke with the SSLN *comandantes* he left behind a note for Humberto Ortega that was similar to the message Guevara sent to Castro when he went first to Santo Domingo, and Mexico, and then to Bolivia to be murdered: he said that he was neither Sancho nor the Quixote, but he was going off to make new revolutions throughout the Continent. In fact, Pastora knew he was defecting. His message was a clever ruse to avert suspicion, but Ortega and others in the National Directorate knew. It's a wonder he was allowed to escape unharmed.

Once while I was dining in the restaurant Antojitos, Thomás Borge and Pastora entered with a party of heavily armed troops. They took a big table in the corner, their rifles and grenades clinking, and they ordered beer and food.

Pastora seemed uncomfortable among such a company. After a while he got up and went to the washroom and when he came back he stood in the center of the restaurant among the diners, as though preparing to accept their homage, or ovations. I had finished my meal and paid up, so I went over and shook the hand of this "fortunate soldier."

"The last time I saw you in person," I said, in Spanish, "was at the National Palace."

"Thank you very much," Pastora said.

"That was a great day," I said.

"I'm not surprised," Pastora said.

He kept staring away from me at the back of Borge, bent over his stew, and nothing he said made any sense at all. Nothing followed. He was plainly uncomfortable about speaking within earshot of the Interior Minister.

I said, "I wish you good health and good fortune."

"Unfortunately, you probably do," Pastora said, in English, and moved away from me back to his colleagues who were still at the table.

Pastora said he was "deeply honored" when they told him that your CIA never trusted him. Well it's all right to be gallant, but you also have to be smart. Pastora was just a big cowboy. He called Tacho Somoza "the last marine." What was he — the eighth pillar of wisdom?

On the Bay Islands once, which are Honduran, I saw a Nicaraguan fishing boat which they say was commandeered by Pastora's people. It had two cannon shots above the water line. It was beached, and the Hondurans lost one of their own boats to the Nicas when this damaged boat drifted toward their shore.

I asked a local Garufino about the boat and he said,
"Pastora used it to go shark fishing. The sharks bit those
holes in the boat."

"He thought he had more lives than a cat," said this
black man, "and then came the day they almost blew him
away. He said it was your CIA. It could have been the
Sandinistas too. They took a big mister and they made him
look stupid. Too much ego; the communists have discipline. They don't get caught with their pants down, looking silly. People say they mean, but not silly."●

ROLEX (1981)

This is the story of Obregon Kent. When he stood in the shadows of the overhang at night in the Plaza de España, he liked to refer to himself as "Max Factor" because of the dark red lipstick he daubed across his mouth. He was born near the Río Coco of Garufino parents.

He'd come to Managua in '73 to work on a stall in the Eastern Market, but he was a pretty boy in those days and easily noticed. There was the earthquake, and by 1978 he was living with an aide to Howard Hughes in one of the colonias in a big house with a black marble bathtub, not very far from the Chief of Police.

"Pan dulce," he called that time, though "there were certain indignities. . . ." Max Factor explained his lover did not allow him any spending money, but he was encouraged to steal jewelry from the man's mother, who lived in a separate wing of the mansion.

Even so, Max Factor didn't really welcome the victory; his lover left Nicaragua and the mansion was confiscated. He took to the streets, became a *puto*. His pickups called him "Rolex." "It wasn't much of a life," as he told the Maryknolls in Sandino City when they took him in overnight. He was later tested for AIDS and told he was not ill, but could be a carrier. He was to keep his trade off the streets.

For a while he worked on a road gang building the highway to the East Coast, but he was used to a much softer life, or, at least, a life without calluses and backaches, and he drifted back to Managua and met Prudhomme one dark night, for whom he promised he would do wonderful things if my friend would let him come back to his hotel room. "I am a married man," my friend claims he said.

"Most of my clientele are," Max Factor replied.

"I don't even like boys," my friend said then.

"Brother," said Obregon, "when I reached manhood I also reached womanhood. Have no doubts about me." All this and more he told my friend as they stood in the darkness of the overhang and watched the police patrols circle the city. Prudhomme said he walked away finally and did not expect to see this *negrito* again, but the next evening the concierge paged him in the bar to say a fellow was asking to see him.

Prudhomme said, "Order me another drink." Then he went to meet this visitor.

When he was gone a few minutes I went to the door and peered through the etched glass into the lobby. Prudhomme was standing in front of a slim-waisted black man with reddish-brown hair, cherry red lips. This fellow looked like a production overrun of the capitalist system, for he was wearing a chartreuse polo shirt across which Yves St. Laurent had scrawled his signature, and his tight-fitting jeans bore the stitched autograph in orangy-gold thread of an aging society deb who was now a chic designer.

Prudhomme seemed to be taking his measure of the man's intentions by weighing something shiny against the open palm of his hand. Presently his palm closed into a fist, and I saw my friend wag his finger and then reach into his pocket and remove a few bills and hand them to the man.

The fellow's lips moved: whether in thanks, or to curse I could not be sure.

When Prudhomme came back he told me all that he knew about Max Factor. He said the man had traced his whereabouts by asking the concierge about the Frenchman staying in the hotel. He had a request to make. He had an opportunity to leave Nicaragua on a Taca flight that very evening. He needed money, of course, and he wasn't begging. He still had a small gold ornament from his old lover that was worth quite a lot, he believed, and if Prudhomme would trade with him for dollars he would not have to go to the state bank and be cheated.

Prudhomme told me, "I have no idea what I shall do with a solid gold ring in the shape of a foreskin, but it must surely be worth two hundred dollars if it's worth a penny."

He clanked the ring down on the table. It was heavy — 18-carat gold, worked in the Italian style, so that every wrinkle and fissure in the surface of this rather large, ornate prepuce with its shiny thin retractable gold skin could be seen.

"Sucker," I told him.

"Perhaps I'll meet a girl sometime who'd like this as a gift," he smirked.

I said, "That would be quite something to have to live up to."

"Of course," he said, "I'll have it sterilized first."

From that day on, Prudhomme began to wear the ring as a kind of good luck charm. It caused a certain amount of comment. Women usually were offended. It was on his hand the day we went to Boaca to look at the Soviet tanks. Some charms bring you more luck than others. Some months after Prudhomme went back to Europe I saw the same ring on the finger of one of Arce's men. How he got it I never have known. Perhaps his lover worked in the hospital where they chopped my friend's hand. ●

MARCO IN VERMONT (1984)

"Now everybody I know is a Contra," Marco greeted me when his bus pulled away. We were standing beside his one battered leather suitcase under cool green Vermont shade.

A bulky man, he gave me a small man's look — pleading, heartbroken, open-eyed, watery. "It's very complicated. I don't mean they like the *gringos* because they don't. But every Nica . . . and if I am not," he flirted with some shadows on the ground, "it's really not because I remain loyal to this government. If I were that loyal, I wouldn't be here with you now in Vermont."

We'd hardly embraced, no small talk, quick furtive looks appraising our weight, our health, our sobriety, then: "The war was such a long time ago, Rik. Now I believe only in myself and my friends, and I hope you are still my friend."

After a year of silence, he'd rung me up first thing, from the Miami Airport, having just cleared Immigration and Customs.

"Enemy of Humanity? It's your friend Marco."

"Marco *qué tal!*"

"*Bien,* . . . and how's our friend Nikelus," he asked right away of another writer I'd introduced him to. "How you are doing, Rik, old sport? Very pleased to hear from me I'm sure."

As though I'd just dialed Marco in Masaya, or would, or could, he went on, "I'm cherry pip myself."

When he's drinking, Marco puts on some of the airs of a Brit from Patagonia, or the Falklands. He'd lived a year in B.A., Argentina's Brit colony, in exile, when he was writing and publishing his first book.

Now he's telling me about conditions in his home town of Masaya, where we first met and I have visited him many

times: the beautiful Masaya of his poems, Masaya torched
and bombed where he and I have seen many a good man
and woman suffer.

"Masaya, city of guitars," he wrote once. Now he says:
"There are even lines to snoop on other people in Masaya
these days. Rik, the biggest business is what you call other
peoples'."

"Bigger than the hammock trade?"

"Surely."

I try to keep him jabbering so I can learn what he's
doing in the States, and why now. All he says is, "That's
my friend, Rik, that's the spirit. *Pura Nica . . . casi
Nicaraguense.* (Almost a Nicaraguan)."

"How is Mauricio?" I ask, about another former insur-
gent and friend who, at last report, was a Sandinista magistrate. I had been expecting them both to leave for quite
some time. "Is his son fighting?" I ask.

"Which boy?"

"The son of Mauricio. Carlos — the *rubio.*"

"Rik," he says, "when your best friend works for the
government you stop talking about your kids."

Marco is a hero of the Revolution, a once-well-regarded
poet and protegé of the "greats." Coppery-skinned — an
Indian, he always insists.

"In Managua at night," he now says, "nobody is reading
Vicente Alexandre. But everybody's lover sleeps with a
comandante, boys first, and even the aides, you must please
forgive me, have AIDS."

"That bad?"

"Not if you like boys."

One of his ancestors had been a brown-skinned president of the Republic during the nineteenth century, when
there was actually a brief federation of the States of Central
America. He speaks Nahuatl and German, French, a ver-
sion of the Sioux dialect, and has ladino-speaking relatives.
"Nowadays," he tells me, "we're all becoming agronomists,

so now all the eggs have double yolks, and when you crack them open they stink double, too."

"Seguro?"

I sometimes wonder if Marco exaggerates.

"You won't like the water down there any better than me old sport I'm sure, old cock. Too many sharks, Rik. You know."

He's turned in his gun, gone back to newspaper editing, writing, graphics, but he's refused to join "the process." Never openly critical, except among his friends until his newspaper was closed down.

Over the phone now, Marco says, "I don't deny we made up stories. If we told the truth they would certainly kill us."

"What will you do in the States?"

"I have friends."

"What sort of people?"

"Wouldn't you like to know? Actually, Rik, my brother, all the best Nicas are in California. I'll be going there soon and then we'll see if it doesn't work out, one way or the other."

I ask why he doesn't say more.

"Because I don't want you to worry about me now," he says. "It's very complicated but I'm not worried anymore, really. Now I will travel here and yon."

"Have *yoni* will travel."

He isn't laughing, more like bringing up phlegm.

"Come to Vermont," I offer then. It's my very first opportunity.

"Vermont?" He seems to be considering an array of important invitations "here and yon," though first he must recall the name and the place. "It's the birthplace of Robert Frost?"

"He's buried nearby for sure."

"Then I'll come; we Nicas can't afford the road not taken."

"Be sure to bring along your spring peepers."

"Rik, old cock," he sighs.

The next time Marco calls he tells me what bus I am to meet. "You will not believe Nicaragua, Mr. Rik," he tells me. "We're all marching together into the volcano."

We're drinking rum over ice in a dark bar near the bus terminal. Though the room is yeasty cool, Marco sweats a lot. His head looks as though he's bottled himself in clear glass, a brow as sweated as a jar in a fridge. Each glance a throwaway. No deposit, no return. "The boys still giving you a hard time?" I ask.

"The boys." He pretends to spit. "*Patria Libre,* when they pick our pockets."

I point out my country hasn't exactly been helpful.

"Your president has a cancer." He claps a hand to his mouth to silence himself, and peers around in the gloom. "I should not talk against those who give me refuge. You know your country, Rik, but Nicaragua is now my . . . *destiny.* So I'm out the front door."

Through the smoke from his cigarette, his words seem loud, oracular. He seems to be listening to himself like a censor and peers out again, as though expecting immediate arrest, an official reproach.

"I never believed I would believe the things I believe now," he announces. "Let me tell you a joke I heard in Matagalpa. One night our leader Danilo Ortega exhibits himself to his wife, Rosario. She's a very ambitious woman, no, as we all know, a regular *arriviste,* so she says 'fancy that,' and suggests he talk to the Russians about acquiring an armored extender cap. So he makes an appointment with the new Soviet Ambassador and shows him just what he's got. You know. '*Cosa maravillosa,*' the emissary declares, 'but in Third World terms, as these things now stand, it seems a little insignificant. You should see Fidel's.' Danilo goes back to Rosario. 'The Russians say

I should see Fidel's. Mine is relatively insignificant.' 'Don't listen to the flatterers,' she says. 'They're just being diplomatic.' "

"There must be lots of jokes like that in Nicaragua nowadays," I say, when he waits for me to laugh.

"Rik, you were with us once. You should know."

I've known him since 1978. He saved my life, offered me a Scotch in his studio above the blazing marketplace afterwards. Now, in this bar, I know he isn't planning to go back home again to Masaya. His fear makes my heart race. I know I have nothing to go back to either. With Marco in exile, Nicaragua is just another place. I ask where's Mauricio? Will he be staying on?

"He's in the business now, Rik. Sure I like the States, sure a lot," he says. "But I'm no *gringo*. *Zapatero a tus zapatos.* I am *pura Nica* and someday maybe . . . no . . ." He stops himself again, his hands up to his face, and slumps suddenly supine with his head against the table. He seems to be quaking slowly, softly. Drunk.

He won't be going back. I'm sure of that.

"Our friend Mauricio had many highly placed friends." He speaks into his hands. "Consequently we're no longer such good friends."

His face has an odd clown-white cast when he glances up again. "I'm just an old *hidalgo* Rik," he adds, "and I can't get used to the way things are done among so-called friends nowadays."

I've written Marco every week over the last nine months, but he swears it has been at least that long since he received any mail from me. "WHO IS READING MY LETTERS?" he announces to the bartender across the way wiping out glasses. The man smiles, as who should say, and we're asked if we want another round.

When the fresh drinks arrive Marco lifts his glass: "To liberty, which is the fruit of Revolution, according to Mr. Vargas Llosa. The tree is all bare."

He downs it all in one big gulp. He isn't going back for sure. He really can't afford to retire on a welfare check in Miami and if he goes back they'd arrest him for public drunkenness. "I ain't a coward," he tells me suddenly, and fills his mouth with ice.

There'll be no more drinks for now. Marco is fifty-five, with galloping diabetes aggravated by rum. He's really not cut out for writing gossip about Sunrise Park, or one of those other Nica suburbs of Miami, for the Cuban press— the only work he might be getting here in the States, once his new friends in California tire of his politics. One of his daughters had been left behind with her young draft-age husband. His mistress has gone off with a young *cumpa* and later has denounced him in *Sábado,* the literary pages of the Party newspaper. He complains of blackouts. Going back is sure death, which probably isn't very far away, I think, in any case.

He says, "Perhaps I will be a quartermaster again, as I was against old Somoza."

"On which side?"

"With the People," he says, smirking a little.

"Rik, it gets worse and worse," he says. Hardly any better, to his way of thinking, for the *campesinos.*

So now he sits opposite me, like a large metal statuary bust to all the times of prison and torture under the old regime, and the shrapnel wound in his leg which still makes him limp. My intercepted letters to Marco only confirm feelings that have propelled him to Miami and safety—that the government suspects him of collusion with the enemy "sell-outs." He can surely never go back now.

I say, "I hope you are not in any trouble."

"Do you think," he asks, "I am of that sort?"

"You tell me."

He's silent. "Too many people are dying already," I say, "especially in the North."

"They send civilians where there are mines," he replies.
"My government does that. They want martyrs. The
Contra fights just like the Sandinista used to fight in the
old days."

"Is that really true, Marco?"

"It don't matter. Nicaragua treats all of us the same now,
it's bad, — but they say we are doing this to preserve our
freedom."

Once again he laughs, that harsh phlegmy paroxysm.

He's so drunk he has blacked out on his feet by the time
I get him home to my place where he'll be staying a while.
With a belch and a cough, Marco greets my wife as though
he were doing a screen test as stand-in for Victor
McLaughlin. "Good night," she says. He goes straight up
the stairs to bed.

The next morning he's up early preparing coffee with
Nicaraguan rum for my wife, whom he calls "Alicia."

"It's too early in the morning Marco, please," she says.

I go off to the bathroom and come back again to hear
Marco teasing Alicia about all my alleged affairs with
Nicaraguan women.

"You know that isn't true," I say from the doorway in
my robe.

"It's joking, Rik. What difference anyway?" He sips
white rum straight. "You are a man . . . and they were
womens."

My wife looks very cross. "He's drunk rather early for
today," she announces. Putting a thread through a needle,
she almost pricks her fingertip and quickly sucks on the
finger anyway.

"In Nicaragua," Marco says, "some men still do as they
wish sometimes, you know."

"Viva Nicaragua Libre," I say.

"I didn't mean that, Rik—Rik, *please.*" His face looks
stricken, pained, grave.

That evening we're all invited to a dinner party. I still have some work to do at my desk before we can go. I tell Marco I will work only a little while and then maybe we will all take a swim at the lake before dressing for dinner.

He follows me through the alcove into my studio and stands above me while I pretend to get busy.

"We all made mistakes," he says, "errors of judgment. Terrible. You *periodistas* are no less culpable. We never should have trusted those delinquents. I also am guilty because I trusted them, and even fought beside them. They exploited our courage, our hopes."

"I can still hear you telling Mauricio, Marco," I recall. " 'I personally could live with the communists easier than with old Somoza and his whores.' "

His face turns red: "I don't say they're communists. I say they are whores."

"It doesn't make any difference now," I say. "The thing is to avoid more killing."

"Maybe so. Maybe not." He shrugs at me, as though to cast this sad silly look from off his face, like a mask. "What we avoid they do anyway, Rik."

I turn in my chair to face him.

"What good will more bloodshed do?"

"Oh, let's just be nice to the *cabrones,* and they'll surely return the compliment?"

"Not exactly Marco."

"What do you know?" he demands. "Why should you care?"

His eyes have started to tear and turn red, as though he's never quite sobered up from the night before.

He says, "Your friends are losing this war, *hermano,* so, of course, they are now the enemy . . . But when we took you into our homes and sheltered you . . ."

"I tried to be an honest friend . . ."

". . . But you were never really one of us. You were just a journalist. Now I ask you, why should I leave Nicaragua?

I'll probably never go back, but why am I leaving? Me? Your brother? Why?"

"To save your own life," I say. "Nothing better than that."

Marco stares at me coldly. "I don't wish to be a security guard in Miami," he announces in a very loud voice. "Not me, mister, never!"

"Would you like to be our Secretary of State?" I ask, angrily.

"So now we are all Contras," Marco says again, "and all you Yankees," he adds, "even you too, *hermano,* are just as Dario described them: with Anglo Saxon eyes and barbaric souls."

Somehow my last Nicaraguan friend has gotten himself very drunk and seems about to pass out: "I will not deal with you any more."

He falls against a chair.

"Later," I tell him, softly. But his eyes are closed, a look of the most serene rage on his face. He's soon asleep and snoring at my back as I turn away to work, if even for a little while.

Marco is awake and sober within two hours and then drunk again within two more, just in time for the party.

He borrows one of my short jackets, washes, shaves, but seems feverish and besotted, sloppy with his words, clumsy on his feet. He nearly tips over my writing desk when he collides with it; and when I grab him so he won't fall, the shrubby sting of my expensive aftershave seems to saturate his face and costume.

In the car he tells us, abruptly, "They talk about the infant mortality rate going down, but it's going up, you know, like a SAM-7 rocket."

The conservative Vermonters we're visiting welcome him as our friend, their guest. He is also the exotic stranger they're all interested, initially, in interviewing over a drink, a canapé. Marco takes advantage of the situation: "I come from the country of the volcano which breeds parrots," I overhear him telling one woman, "where the trees produce ipecac which you use sometimes to make you vomit."

He's equally sententious over cold sherry soup about how to prepare a proper gazpacho, about the spondee in *Spanish* poetry, then compliments our hostess on the soft extent of her bosoms, and, finally, almost is the cause of a sexual civil war breaking out openly when he becomes attracted to (and goes after) one partner of a longstanding lesbian couple.

"You are such a rose," he tells her out loud, declaring his skepticism next about her sexual orientation, complimenting her on her ladylike airs, the shape of her hands and her body, her true sexual needs which he, as an expert on women of all classes, understands only too well, until Riorden says, with angry disdain, "Lookit man, fuck off!"

"She don't mean what you say," Marco replies. "It's playacting. Not normal for a woman, and I can tell you are a true woman, for sure."

"And that's why I like girls, grease-puss."

Riorden turns to me with a look which begins to implore, though only to cover over homicidal intentions: "Who dug up Romeo here?"

"Oh, she's only a big tease-it," Marco says.

"Frankly I doubt that," I tell him.

"Richard, please," my wife says.

"This woman needs some good Nicaraguan beef—a *churrasco*," Marco adds.

"Watch it there, Bosco," Riorden says. She has her dukes up.

My wife also is furious with Marco and, of course, with me, his friend. To pacify her I turn on him: *"Hermano,"* I tell my friend, hoping to intervene before there's mayhem, "it's very late and you look dog tired and you've also overindulged."

"Borracho," he says. Drunk.

"Probably just jet lag," I explain to Riorden and her girlfriend. I put my arm around Marco and lead him heavily out with me past our hostess, toward the car.

He's mumbling, "Good evening, señora, the pleasure was all shit."

In good shape Marco can shoot the eye out of a vulture with a Belgian carbine at fifty yards in one squeeze. Now he's shooting off a clip at a time, and mostly missing. "Fucking Marxist lesbians," he roars as we drive off. "DOWN WITH MARXIST LESBIANISM."

When I come downstairs in the morning he's up, waiting for me to brew more fresh coffee.

"No rum this time," he swears. "It's a promise."

"How could I do what I did last night?" he asks suddenly.

"Well don't worry about it."

"How can I not?"

"You weren't really in love with Riorden were you?" I ask. "Weren't you just trying to get lucky?"

"Lucky —," he laughs. "During the war I was different. One made friends with women quickly and well . . . I love my wife, Rik," he adds, "but I am not, you know, a celibate monk."

"I guess you've just been out of circulation lately."

"Doña Inez, my wife, understands these things," he adds. "She'll be meeting me in California, you know. She knows how terrible things are. I haven't even felt like a man."

"How does a man feel?" I ask. "Tell me, Marco."

Much of my morning has been wasted. Aside from my work, I have shopping to do, and cooking later. There's the child to be picked up after camp. My own need is to get to my desk and sit staring into space.

Marco says, "I'm shy. Please, Rik."

He doesn't say more.

When coffee is ready, I go with my cup into my room. "You still don't understand," he says, following me. "Here we are all terrified. Something must be done. Why should I be so scared in my own country, Rik?"

I have nothing reassuring to tell him. He's right, of course, though I can't support his cause, even if I were sure what he was up to, or who his new friends are.

"Scruples come easily to the Anglo Saxon," Marco says. "He needs them as he picks our pockets."

"Then you must not choose us to be your allies, *compañero*" I reply.

"Please rid me and my children forever of these delinquents," he says.

"Hooligans," I correct him. "Somoza used to call them that—and so did Sagetario, the torturer."

"Well they weren't always wrong," Marco says.

"I'm sorry you feel that way," I tell him, "awful sorry."

He takes nothing more to drink in my house for as long as he's with us. That evening he packs his bag and announces he will go by bus the next morning to an old school friend in Missouri.

With his bag next to him, he stands in our hall early the next morning, and shakes my wife's hand. It's raining hard outside. "Someday we will invite you both back."

"Maybe we'll come if you invite us," I say, "*Suerte, Marco.*"

"Of course."

"Good luck," my wife says. "Please take care of yourself and Doña Inez."

"And don't shoot unless you can see the whites of their eyes." I tell him.

We stand another moment. Lit by the overhead fixture, his brow seems burnished bright, his cheekbones coppery and dark-shadowed, where he has just doused himself with more scent. "Enemy of Humankind," he smirks, "I shall truly miss you . . . But," his glance is distant, "here we

see, in Vermont, the limits of our friendship. *Adios."*
"*Adio,* Marco."

I say goodbye to my good friend who is now, unfortunately, my enemy.●

WITH BRAVO IN RIVAS (1979)

Commander Bravo wore riding boots and jodhpurs, carried a crop, had small waxed mustaches, and a .45 Smith & Wesson in a tooled leather holster. Under the shade of an almond tree, on the outskirts to Rivas, just beyond a sandbagged .50-caliber gun emplacement, he interrupted his urination to glace up at me and say: "Someday you will permit me to buy you a Scotch in Tegucigalpa."

He pronounced "Scotch" to rhyme with "coach," with a hearty Anglo-Spanish accent of upper class affectation. Then he commenced to button his fly.

"Why would I wish to go to Tegoo?" I asked.

"Buena clima," he smirked. "Good weather. Brrisk," he added, with a Scottish burr, and laughed. His real name was Pablo Emilio Salazar; Somoza called him "Gallant." A month later he was dead in Tegoo after being lured by his abandoned mistress, who had been coerced to work for the Sandinistas, to a rendezvous at a small hotel. But that afternoon, just before Rivas, he seemed very much alive.

"I have half the Sandinista military bottled up here," he said. "The great hero Cero, Eden Pastora, is virtually my captive."

"True," I said, "you have him stalled, but Somoza has fled and the FSLN junta is in Managua making law. Just what do you hope to gain by holding out?"

"A little more time," Bravo said.

He finished buttoning himself and walked toward the machine gun.

I followed him.

Right then a Pastora battery started angling mortar shells which straddled the grove of trees we were near. Bravo was a brave man, if a bit foolhardy. He told his troops not to seek cover but to dig themselves into the earth "with asses and elbows."

The gunner took a piece of shrapnel on his face.

"How much more time?" I screamed, with my head sideways in the dirt.

"A little more," Bravo said.

The shelling ceased. I went back to my car and left him. "Remember," he called after me. "Johnnie Walker Black."

"I hate Scotch," I shouted back as I drove off.

In Tegoo he was murdered gruesomely and locked inside a shack, left to rot in the baking heat for days. No way to treat a spiffy and gallant officer of the line, but he was also a killer who'd trained in the Canal Zone with the green berets at Fort Gulick, and in Italy. As one Sandinista *comandante* later said, "If Bravo had lived the Contras would have had a leader. Now they have only businessmen and racketeers. Gangster armies are easily defeated, but one brave man can get much from his soldiers. Bravo had to die. He was the U.S. ace in the hole."

He stood slightly bandy-legged beneath that almond tree, and snapped that riding crop down hard against the open palm of his hand. It was a hot July afternoon. Much of the countryside was already peaceful, after thousands of deaths. Bravo was determined to keep the war going. I later learned his holding action was intended to keep the Sandinists from entering the nearby port of San Juan Sur where a couple of hundred or more of Somoza's Guardia were being evacuated in barges to drift up the Gulf of Fonseca toward La Union, Salvador.

Was he also thinking of his mistress he would soon leave behind in Nicaragua after evacuating his wife and children?

"No problems," Bravo told his machine gunner, as though allowing us to pass to a forward position was his personal act of magnanimity. He tossed back his head, again repeated how he would like someday "to take a Johnnie Walker" with me. He survived Rivas, but in Tegoo he was tricked, ambushed, and tortured. Dead men often seem foolish for failing to be prudent when they die before their time.

The sentimental gesture Bravo made in going to meet his mistress resulted in his murder. "We are fighting for our wives and mothers," he told me that day in Rivas. "Hearth and home," he added in barely intelligible English.

Bravo had many vanities and faults; lack of loyalty was not one of them. He was a sentimental murderer, surprised by assailants who did not doubt he would come to desire his mistress again, once he'd satisfied his obligations as *paterfamilias.*

"These people we are fighting," he told me in Rivas, "have a cause just as I have a cause. I do not mind dying for my family."

("And my mistress," he should have added.)●

PALMEROLLA (1983)

It happened on the streets of San Pedro Sula. I wanted to see the huge American air base at Palmerolla on the road to Tegucigalpa, and in San Pedro, in the United Fruit Company district of Honduras, it was early morning when I found a driver who would be willing to take me there for a generous consideration. "I could also show you many of the so-called Contras in their camps," he said, but I'd seen enough of them. We decided to look in on Palmerolla, with a brief side trip to the ruins of Copan; and, as he was an agreeable fellow and liked to chat, I sat up front with him in order to practice my Spanish.

"We are the Nation of the '70s," a reformist Honduran president once boasted: "70 percent illiteracy, 70 percent poverty, 70 percent rural." I'd hoped we might talk about such things, or about politics, as we went along, but my driver was mostly interested in talking about the rich, and about women. The very rich in Honduras, he said, were almost always Jews. Like this Mr. Goldsmith of the Atlantic Bank. My driver was quite convivial about all he said, even as he told me about the other rich Jew who owned a lot of Honduras, "Meester Rockefeller."

I had to assume he was some sort of leftist, with more grudge than militancy or politics, else he would not have otherwise volunteered to be so conspicuous around Palmerolla.

"*Compañero*," I suggested grandly. "Let's stop for coffee somewhere."

"Around here we say *hermano* just to be friendly," he corrected me. "It's much safer."

It was such a fine day when it began and together we saw much of Mayan Copan. He proved a knowledgeable guide, whether or not he was telling the truth—a true storyteller.

Of the new invaders of the U.S. Air Force, whom we observed from a hillside overlooking the huge busy base, which seemed to have been bulldozed out of terraced fields and rain forest, he remained silent, noncommital, except to advise me that the Military Police could be difficult about taking pictures. "I don't travel with a camera," I said. "Just my memory."

"Intelligent," he commented. Or perhaps, "Intelligence." I wasn't listening very carefully.

It was dark by five thirty when we started back over the mountain roads. Again I was up front with the driver, and I noticed the headlights behind us almost immediately. They kept their distance, though, from pass to pass, and all the small towns and junctions and then the paltry shabby suburban subdivisions; for the Central American poor are also crowding toward the large cities for opportunity, just as they come here to the States; and it seemed that evening as though the soldiers in the vehicle behind us were not so much pursuing as escorting us, all the way back to San Pedro Sula.

It was toward the end of the dinner hour when we entered San Pedro and the stalls and restaurants all seemed very busy. I asked to be dropped off in the principal square and paid the previously agreed sum. "Someday you introduce me to Gloria Steinem," my driver shouted as he moved off, with my hand still on his door; and when I turned right, the Jeep which had been trailing us all that time pulled up and parked alongside me. There was a driver in front and two heavily armed noncoms in the back, an empty jump seat, a field radio with a big antenna.

Honduran or U.S., I couldn't tell who they were for sure, and they seemed to eye me as though I was clearly not who I seemed to pretend I was.

Dressed in U.S. style camouflage fatigues, with forager style caps, all three wore Spanish name tags on their chests, though the younger noncom in the back, with more rank, was much fairer complected than I and spoke without any accent. "Please get in," this man, Rivera, told me. I didn't argue. I sat in the jump seat. He had an Uzi with a very short metal stock on his lap.

They all seemed to know I was a tourist. At first, they didn't ask to see credentials. As we drove off one said, "You smell bad."

"I was out in the country all day," I explained. "It was very hot. I'm a journalist."

We were going around the square and nobody was listening to me. The second time around Rivera asked if I had visited a certain book store when I was in Tegucigalpa.

Of course I had.

"Did you meet any poets?" he asked.

In fact I had, and one had signed a copy of his book for me, *Los Pobres.*

"The poor," Rivera seemed to be repeating my words for his friends. "The offenses against them here are numerous and you are the one to help them of course, you and this poet."

His behavior toward me was no more threatening than that, a smirk in the dark, and then we started up from where we had stopped, alongside a market kiosk, and around that square again, a route which we would circumnavigate at least fifty times.

"You should meet our *coronel,*" Rivera laughed. "He has a reputation among the poor — especially the refugees in the camps. He would enjoy you."

They had stopped again, and the driver was pouring out small cups of coffee from a thermos, which they drank quickly, without offering me any. Then they admitted they'd followed me all the way from Palmerolla and wanted to know why I'd even gone there.

"Because I'm a journalist."

"And your driver? He is a journalist, too?"

"You know, he's from Guatemala," his companion said.

"Did you know that?" I was asked. I confessed I did not.

"Like so many refugees here," he added.

"We saw you both this morning in Camayagua taking coffee."

"That's news to me," I told Rivera.

"Why would he want to take you to Palmerolla?" Rivera asked. "He doesn't even belong."

"Because," I replied, "I asked him to, and I paid."

We never made any more progress than that. I was asked the same questions twenty or more times. I was asked why I was interested in such people. I was asked by Rivera, specifically, what did I know about this man I'd chosen to be my driver, who could be Guatemalan, or even a Salvadorean.

Really, I knew nothing about Carlos except what they told me.

We drove around the square again. I was beginning to feel dizzy from the sudden lurching of hard left turns.

It seemed people on the streets were beginning to notice us. Surely they would not harm me now.

I asked to be released.

"Soon," was all Rivera said.

They alternated being bullying and sly. The same questions asked again, and then again, and now finally they asked to see my press credentials. "You look very important, meester," one said.

"I just work for a living," I said.

"Meester Worker," Rivera said.

Then we lurched forward toward the entrance of my hotel; the door swung open, and I was given the high sign to leave. "Well, brother," Rivera said to me, "no more of this important work for you. I believe you will be leaving San Pedro tomorrow."

And so I did, as early as possible.●

ALBERTO Y SYLVIA (1986)

In the lounge, in the Hotel Sula Deluxe, Alberto y Sylvia shake their tambourines around and around to the movements of their rear ends as they sing *Guantanamero:* red *boleros,* white peasant blouses, tight satin trousers, black flamenco boots, a happy couple in black light, faces scorched with ecstasy.

"Yo soy un hombre sincero," and Alberto's voice soars and breaks like in adolescence, and then Sylvia has to pick him up the scale again with her husky cajoleries.

The lounge is nearly empty, and frosty with air conditioning. A bartender shakes piña coladas to serve at the conclusion of their set. Alberto lifts his electric guitar off the bandstand so that the pigtail uncurls. He will sing Beatles, at the request of Colonel Azucar of the 6th Brigade. She will sing *Paloma Negra* for the Colonel's date. *Volaré. Vecina Mare! La Vie En Rose.* A jet stream of melodies, jettisoned from the pop discs of Mexico, Cuba, Italy, the States. This is Honduras, an international cabaret. They close with *"Solemente Una Vez"* in two-part harmony, Sylvia imitating Linda Ronstadt.

The applause afterwards is light and scattered and the room remains dark. At their usual table, Alberto and Sylvia smoke Marlboros, and they are sweating, a fudge of brown makeup. As usual, they are talking about New York, where they have never been. It was not by mistake that they went south from Miami rather than north eighteen months ago: Merida, Villahermosa, Belize City, Puerto Barrio, a circuit. They've played the best joints, such as they are in Central America, to put a high gloss on their Hispanic "act."

"You sang too loud, you drown me out," says Sylvia, dark-haired, fair, between quick breaths. With her pale, heavy arms crossed on the table, she shows a wholesome plumpness, except for her smile which is sour, disapproving. "Gotcha," Alberto replies. "Next time I promise *una poca voce fa.*"

"Forget it." She lights up again. Alberto watches her, his belly jammed against the table edge so he can't close his bolero. He hopes she sees the smile he has only for her beneath his thinning hair, worn in a crown, a sort of modified Beatle look. His family came from the Abruzzi. He has the forthright pout of a Roman senator. For what it's presently worth, which is very little, he adores Sylvia. Alberto says, "Darling, nobody in Sula gives two shits for us. If we stay here when the season moves to Merida, we'll get so fat people will think we made a baby together."

"There's not gonna be no babies," Sylvia says. "When you make me shake up there on the stand, it don't make me want to have no babies."

They speak English. The only Spanish they know are song lyrics, the names of different foods, and things to drink and smoke.

"I'm tired, too," Alberto says, "but we got one more set before closing time. You want food?"

She shakes out her dark lacquered hair. No food.

"You want smoke?"

"I had enough," Sylvia says. She tells Alberto, for maybe the third time, how she promised her mother to be home for Rosh Hashonah. It may be her father's last year on Earth. He has liver cancer.

Alberto says, "We got maybe 900 lemps stashed with Vidas. Two more weeks we could make it, but we'll be awful goddamn poor."

"I doubt if I could take two more weeks of this. Central America makes me feel so dumb . . . You were just gonna get your shit together."

"*We,*" he reminds her.

"*We,*" she repeats.

"Anyway," he says," I guess it's a dumb act."

"Vidas doesn't think so."

"What do I care what Vidas thinks?"

"He feeds us, pays us," she reminds him.

"Yea,—well maybe," he says, "we ought to be a little more individualistic, maybe bring back "Havanagila" and the other Jewy stuff. It might liven things up a little."

"Maybe," she smiles like lean bacon. "We should just go home and try something else."

They have a conversation like this almost every night since they came to the Isthmus, and almost every night Alberto won't give in. He says, "The Colonel has been here before. He seems to like us."

"Maybe he thinks you're a communist," she says. "He's checking you out."

Alberto orders a second round, which is not on the house. He'll sign the tab. Maybe if business picks up the management will forget.

Maybe they'll go outside when their final set is finished and see the northern lights this far south, or Alberto's brother will send that money order they've been expecting. Then he could buy her some lines, if she wanted any. Maybe Vidas supplies her on the sly. Personally he's stayed clean of toot since Puerto Barrios when they almost got arrested, and God knows what—if not for Vidas's friend Don Pepe, the *patrón*.

He asks, "Why don't we do the Chiquita song?"

"Chiquita banana? That's a commercial, not a song," she reminds him.

"But the business people like it here—Don Pepe liked it."

"You see any Don Pepes here? Any business people?" she asks. "Face it, you're not Julio Iglesias and I'm not Streisand."

"Some really people like us," Alberto says.

"Some people think this hotel is dynamite, too," she reminds him, "because it's clean and cool."

"They doing OK," he says. "We should do that well."

The hotel is so full up they've been moved from their room into the bellmen's quarters in the annex; and tonight all the guests are upstairs in their rooms watching Stateside TV through the hotel's dish antenna. Who can compete with Johnny Carson? David Letterman? Monday Night Football delayed until Wednesday? It's been like this their whole engagement.

Alberto says, "We got twenty minutes till the next show. Let's have something in the coffee shop—a hamburger, some soup, a BLT."

"Maybe a piece of melon," she says, rising heavy, like crepe. Alberto leaves some change for the bartender, and they go out into the lobby toward the coffee shop.

The American Coffee Shop is a chilly underwater blue: tile walls, and chrome counters, dark waitresses in blue pinafores and little starched caps, like nurses' aides. There are see-through plastic drums full of muffins, chocolate cake, a white cake with orange layers; a malted milk machine, a swirling globe of orange juice with a foamy head, and the vapors of CN disinfectant scoured pungently throughout. All that's missing is Archie and the gang. They take a booth near the counter and wait for service.

Two Americans are at the counter eating waffles and syrup. They could be soldiers in civvies, wildcat drillers, agronomists with the fruit company. They wear sand-colored chukha boots. And they're trying to hit on Carmen, who works behind the counter and has three children at home in her shack along the river. She's slicing up papayas with a wop bop a loola of her big knife.

"The night is young, little *señorita*," says one.

The chef, in whites, behind an armory of vats and pots, bangs his spatula loud, like he's playing crazy steel drums. Carmen says, "I don't see no *señoritas* here. You want more *salsa?*"

"She's OK," Alberto says. "I get so tired to hear the same old line of shit thrown at these women, their passivity."

"You haven't improved on it exactly."

Sylvia is doing her lips a dark russet brown, which means she won't have anything but coffee. She asks, "You think what we're doing down here is any better, for that matter?"

"I'm honestly trying to make contact," Alberto says. "I'm not deliberately trying to condescend."

"It don't matter. It's all the same to this broad."

"Who ya kidding with that?" he demands.

She frowns.

She orders coffee and he has a milkshake with an egg, in case he has to drink with the manager and the Colonel afterwards.

Suddenly the pair at the counter spin around on their stools. "You're the singers ay?"

"Yeah," said flatly.

"Americans?" asks the other man. His lips look sticky from syrup. He has a little sandy mustache that droops, big shoulders, a bush jacket.

Sylvia and Alberto nod.

The older man has one of those steel mask faces when he winks roguishly at Sylvia. "Pretty nice."

"Thanks a lot," she says.

"Ay," his friend says, "I caught you the other night and I just want to say you're beautiful. You could be in movies."

"This is my husband, Alberto," Sylvia says. It isn't true they're married, but it saves a lot of explaining and keeps guys away.

The older man says, "We feel like partying. You know of any parties?"

"There's the Liberals and the Conservatives," Alberto says, "and the Communists."

"Very funny."

The younger man, who is quite large, gets off his stool, walks over to where Alberto is tipped backwards in his chair, and pushes him over. "Honey!" Sylvia screams. She's down on her knees. The men are paying the cashier.

"Bastards," she yells. Alberto moans. He likes the cool feel of her hand on his brow. He's not really hurting, but it was a shock, and he's gonna have a bump. Figures he'll stay this way a while longer. See what he'll get. "You alright, Alby?"

"I'm alright," he says.

She says, "Let me help you."

"I'm alright," he repeats.

Lola has his malted on a saucer. He's looking up her skirt. White cotton underpants like a kid's. She's waiting for him to get up.

Alberto grabs the table corner and pulls himself up straight, and then he sits down, dizzy a little, thanks Lola for waiting.

"Cómo no!" she replies. She's off to fetch coffee.

Sylvia asks, "You hurting?"

"Na . . . you know those guys?"

"I saw them in the lounge the other night; I'm sorry about what happened."

"Maybe if you didn't flirt so much," Alberto says.

"I do it as a job," she says, "nothing personal otherwise."

He grunts and takes a big slurp of his milkshake through the straw. The back of his head is hot. Swelling.

"You think you can go on again?"

"You think I can't?"

He gets up and she reaches out to steady him.

"Oh, Alberto," she says, and there's real surprise on her face as Mr. Vidas, the hotel manager, enters the room and heads their way.

He's a small thin dapper man who wears shiny dark suits, and is rumored to carry a piece. On the side, he also changes currencies at better than the official rate. All things considered, he's been nice to Sylvia and Alberto. That they aren't drawing crowds doesn't seem to matter. Somebody's gotta sing in the lounge, and the gringos like to think they can follow the Spanish, so it's better if the singers are gringos also who don't know much Spanish. He told them both once he almost had Vic Damone on the way down.

Now he's standing between Alberto and Sylvia and the counter. "You OK, Alberto?"

"OK."

"I heard what happened. They not guests here; from another place — Canadians."

"It don't matter," Alberto says.

Vidas says. "Some people think Americans are all that way, but they not all. You people always behave real fine, make me proud."

"*Gracias, caballero,*" says Sylvia.

"*Y tu guapa?*" Vidas chucks her under the chin like a patriarch, whispers something to himself in Spanish.

Then he tells them both anyway take the rest of the night off, rest up.

There's a big private party tomorrow night in the lounge and he wants them "all shit shape again."

"*Gracias, exactamente,*" Alberto says. He lets Mr. Vidas take their check and they shake hands *hasta mañana.*

It's twelve fifteen. Sylvia wants to go straight up to bed, but Alberto wants some beers to bring with them. He gets so thirsty at night.

He buys two Salva Vidas, and, when Lola comes with the bill, tells her Vidas is paying for his Vidas tonight, and laughs a little.

Together they go out through the lobby to the back patio and cross over toward their room, which is on the second floor of a wing of motel units, above some garbage cans.

A neighbor dog is baying at the full silvery moon, and rats are scurrying nearby. They enter their quarters, flash on the lights.

"Oh, shit!"

Colonel Azucar's police have been at it again. The room is a shambles. Clothes and letters and "fake books" dumped everywhere. They start picking things up and placing them back where they belong.

"Later," Sylvia says, suddenly, in the middle of all this; and she starts to undress, down to her panties. Her body seems to bloat like dough in the harsh light, but he is aware of his desire, and reaches for her.

"Not now," she says.

"When? It's been weeks and I'm hurting."

"I don't really know." She shrugs him off, goes into the bathroom, runs the shower.

With the water gushing, she starts to sing *"Paloma Negra"* again and her voice is dulcet and rich, and silken, as he's never heard her before.

She sings of her longing, her voice smoky and full, and he has never heard her sing like this anywhere. He knows all about Sylvia and Vidas, and the other men, too—has known forever about that part of Sylvia—, but he still wants her, loves her, he thinks, even so, and now as she sings under the water of a love he has never known with her, he really wants Sylvia more and more. He would love to see her body rouged with the heat she's now feeling, rosy from the beat of the water. And he thinks she still needs him down here in C.A., just as much as he wants and needs her.

"Sylvia," he says. "Baby . . ."

"Somewhere over the rainbow . . .," Sylvia's voice soaring loud and free, in sensual contralto, "Way up high . . ."

"Sylvia," he says, "I'm sorry we're not making it anymore."

"But we never did," she interrupts her song, a face peering out like a bud to reply; and then she yanks the shower curtain tightly shut and commences to sing again, inside the steam of that drenching torrent.

"Dream that I dreamt of . . . once in a lullaby."

When she comes out again, she wears her tangerine wrap, her face soft, childlike. Her cheeks are red, hair hanging limply. She seems a different person, almost virginal.

She finds a cigarette, sits down, crosses her legs so her ample thigh is naked.

"I'm sorry about Vidas," she says. "It's really nothing much."

"I suppose you tell him the same about me," Alberto says.

He's standing over her, with his hands on his hips. He could strike her, caress her.

She glances up, an epicene, almost sluttish glance, eyelash smudging her eyes: "I tell him you are like my brother."

"Thanks a lot."

"Now if you like," she adds, "in a minute we can do it."

"With your brother?" He feels his excitement taking over.

He reaches for her and she gets up and comes to his arms, so warm and wet.

"I hate being here," she says. "Please let's go."

"You'll leave me when we get back."

"No I won't, I promise," she says, and opens her mouth against his.

"I promise."

He has his hands under her wrap. She burns against his fingertips — .

He must have pleased her, for she will not let him go, even afterwards when he's done, and so is she. And when they lie together, with the smoke from their cigarettes rising, she begins to hum, a low throatiness, song he's never heard her sing before.

Elusive melody, erotic *nigun,* song he can never repeat. He tries to hum with her, but always she is somewhere else, and he's croaking by himself until she climbs on top of him again and calls out a name harshly, such as he's never heard before.

"You're hurting me," he tells her then.

"Let's get out of here, please, Alberto," she whispers. "Oh, please soon, Alberto."

"To Miami?"

"And then to New York in a little while."

"And then I'll lose you."

"Not if you still want me." She kisses his neck. "Not if you care enough to get a little better."

"And you?" he asks her. "Will you get better and still care?"

"I am better now," she says, "a very long time. Ever since we came here; I got better right away and I've been waiting for you all the time," and she starts to hum her tune again, and her heat touching his lap where she sits makes him squirm.

She kisses him again and he touches her hair, so soft now, and soon enough she is a heavy liquid splashed against his body and he rises up to meet her and feels his body turn to ice.

"Please — ."

"I'll lose you . . . You'll see."

"Don't be crazy, Alby. I want to go home — back," she adds, "home."

From the plaza, beyond the hotel's front facade, at the municipal bandstand, where the sodium white script of Hotel Sula Deluxe glares against the pepper and gum trees, and even the sky above for some distance, Julio Iglesias sings "Many rivers to cross," and Alberto y Sylvia join in, though somewhat off-key together, and lagging a little behind the tinny noises from the loudspeakers. ●

" . . . corpses are found with both shoes intact. Their clothing on the other hand isn't usable. Ordinarily, it has bullet holes, ... So we don't count on the clothes, but the shoes are like new. . . . they haven't had much wear because their owners haven't been allowed to get very far in life. . . ."

Luisa Valenzuela, as translated by Helen Lane in "Open Door," Selected Stories, North Point Press, 1988.

PART 3

CALAMITY
(A PARABLE)

There was a man in Bonanza who talked only in slogans.

"The People and the Front are one."

"Street cleaning is also a revolutionary act."

He had one son, and when the boy was drafted into the army and killed while on patrol near Jalapa, the man said, "These are times of great sacrifice for everybody."

His wife took sick and there was no proper medicine to cure her. "Women's rights," the man said, "and the national liberation are not the same; neither are they opposed."

There were big food shortages and people like him sometimes felt hungry. "By suffering," he said, "the popular will consolidates."

When his wife died, the man said her life was a "calamity of politics," but later, on his own death bed, he changed his mind and cried out, "Fatherland or Death!"

"A life such as his," said the Cardinal Archbishop, "so exemplary in its ordeal, surely justifies our general anguish."

"In that he was so often wronged this man was right," a liberation priest further declared in eulogy.

On the cross above his grave were inscribed the words of the Chief of State: "We are advancing despite obstacles, despite aggressions, despite calumnies." ●

HYMIE (1987)

Jaime Roldan worked in Government House in Managua. A capable man, easygoing and friendly, he was also a considerable appeaser, always trying to please. We always used to call him "Hymie" and, actually, he seemed to enjoy it. He would say, "If I lived in New York or Miami they would call me that." Such words were said only a little wistfully, as though Jaime might contemplate defecting, if he were not so committed to the "process" in Nicaragua.

In fact, he never really wanted to leave, even when he did. The policies he had to interpret and explain to the press were often obnoxious to him, so he would wheedle and cajole, and sometimes allow just the opposite of what he was supposed to allow. If his Minister was sometimes angry that Jaime could be so easily gotten around, he didn't choose to reprimand him. "It's a good thing he's not a woman," he would say. "Always saying yes the way he does, he would have a terrible repute."

The Minister thought Jaime was loyal, though just a little muddled, and we all thought he was the decent sort who didn't care to be a stickler if he had some human trust in a person. The Jaime we got to know and like had his own view of what he was about. He explained, "People who do what they're told to do are really superfluous. I know all about Party discipline, but in these dangerous times there are enough *hijoputas* without Jaime Roldan."

"That mustn't go over too well with your superiors," I said.

"The People know," he said. "They know who Jaime Roldan is."

He'd fought in Estelí and Matagalpa and had been known for his daring. A friend told me that in October '78 Jaime commandeered a bulldozer and drove it unarmed into a National Guard machine-gun position, crushing the soldiers so that his comrades could advance. When I asked him if he had actually done such a thing, he replied "Other people did things too. That was such a time."

With Jaime I went to Acahaulinca, to see the footsteps of the ancient inhabitants of Nicaragua fleeing the rain of ash from Masaya volcano. There seemed to be some dozen of them in the mud like lava, and those of deer and other large and small animals: my friend said there was some controversy still about how long they had been preserved in mud, some said seven to nine thousand years, and others less.

A feeling of vertigo seized me as I looked down below me. He said, "One feels their fearfulness impressed into this time."

He spoke English poorly, but he could be understood, and he had many friends who were not in the government, even some who were opponents. He'd served right after the victory in San José in the embassy and had left his wife and small child behind when he was called back.

He was a small man with a rather sharp face, and a big wrinkle of bunched skin between his eyes above the bridge of his nose, a kind of worry spot. Jaime lived with a group of *cumpas* in a big house in Colonia Dembach, to which I was never invited, though he was always saying he would someday. He would say, "We have a good cook, and I'm sure you would eat good with us, but I have to ask the others."

That phrase sounded very ominous to me when he said it, and probably it was for him, too, because I never got invited; and when I took him to lunch at the hotel, or at Los Ranchos, he ate ravenously, at my urging, like a man who has not eaten well in a long time. "As good as cook is," he explained, "just the same, it's sometimes nice to take a meal out sometimes, for a change."

Jaime sounded like the husband of some suburban housewife. I figured he was lying about the cook and was down to pretty basic rations, like everybody else in Managua.

"You are always welcome to eat on my expense account," I said.

Smirking, he replied, "Beggar that I am, I humbly thank you."

He was a cultivated man, had translated some of Quevedo, and claimed to have spent his years at university doing nothing but reading Pedro Salinas' great translation of Proust. Once, when I made an inquiry about the family of the foreign minister, he replied in the manner of Proust's narrator: "People who learn some correct detail about another person's life at once draw conclusions from it which are not accurate, and they see in the newly discovered fact an explanation of things that have no connection with it whatsoever."

"That's all very true," I said, "but I was simply asking a question."

"Questions lead to assumptions," Jaime Roldan said.

His manner of reluctance made me admire him all the more. Once at a cocktail party given by the West Germans, which was not unlike certain parties of the Guermantes, Jaime's Minister went out of his way to stop me with a drink in his hand and said, "Roldan says you are a trustworthy person."

"No better endorsement than that," I said.

"Perhaps," the Minister grinned. "Perhaps not."

For a moment he seemed to stand out in the crowded room as sharply as the Rock of Gibraltar stands out from the straits surrounding it, and then he receded again, with a faint wry smile and a little wave of his fingers: *"Ciao Ciao."*

Less than a week later I learned Roldan had been reassigned to the East Coast.

"It's not a promotion," explained Sonia, the niece of a National Guard general who was now foreign news editor of the government press agency.

We were having lunch together in Tiscapa, and I was very aware how she had grown more and more attractive over the years from when I'd first known her when, as a slim waif of a girl, she'd served as an FSLN contact while doing translating for visiting journalists.

I'd always been strongly attracted to Sonia, but I'd heard she was sleeping with one of "the 9" and didn't think I wanted any trouble, so we spoke only about Jaime."

"How long will he have to be in Bluefields?" I asked.

"When he desires change he will be," she said, and, as though being particularly obscure, added, "Jaime never did well with self-criticism."

"But I truly think he is very loyal," I said.

"We'll see," she said. "His boss is no fool."

A few weeks later I got a postcard from Jaime. "Nobody can say who is bluffing who in Bluefields; I am glad the assignment was only temporary."

He told me he'd been sent back "due to ill health" and was presently recuperating at the Hotel at El Transito by the sea. Would I come to visit him sometime in his "Nicaraguan Balbec"? He would make certain I got supper.

I drove out the very next day, but when I got to the hotel they told me Jaime had suffered a "nervous relapse" and was in the hospital in León.

Nicaragua's populated area is small, though the country is large, so I drove to León in a short time and went to the Catholic hospital, which was the only hospital I knew there, and asked after my friend. They said he could not be seen at present, as he was under sedation, but if I came back in the early evening I would probably to able to talk with him.

I hung around León all afternoon, and visited the tombs of Dario and Córtes in the cathedral, and the small museum in a house where Dario was born, and around five went back to the hospital.

Jaime was propped up against some pillows in a ward bed when I arrived. He seemed very weak, as though he could hardly keep his big head from drooping against his shoulders.

"I am so very happy you came to see me," he said. But he didn't look very happy. He looked sadder than any man I'd ever seen. For an hour he just sat there propped up in bed with an IV stuck into his arm and we did not speak, or, rather, I asked him questions, and he did not reply.

I asked what had happened to him? What had Bluefields been like? Did he have plans?

He stared vacantly my way and there were tears clustered in the corners of his eyes.

Then the head nurse came and said I must leave. "Goodbye," I told him. "Be in touch."

"It's all because I have had so much trouble sleeping lately," he said weakly, and closed his eyes again.

I spoke to his boss the following day by phone and was told Jaime was no longer a member of his staff. He would be found other employment, if he was well enough, the Minister pointed out, but it was unlikely that would be in Managua.

"What has happened to him?" I asked. "He seems so different."

"People change," the man said. "These are not good times if one has doubts—and you know he's an insomniac. We have his own words for that."

I did not see my friend before I left Managua. When I invited Sonia to a farewell lunch, she told me Jaime was feeling much better, she had heard, but she would not say where he was, and she would not say much more than that: He was better, and back at work. She hoped I would not write against "the process" in Nicaragua and that I would be coming back someday. That was all she said.

In New York I didn't think of him more than once or twice in passing, a random recollection of some kindness he'd bestowed on me, or others, as I tried to write about that time. He crowded into the miscellany of old events one refers to only for reassurance, but never because one expects to be moved, or instructed.

In December 1985 I made a trip to Miami for a magazine and was entertained by some friends at the jaialai fronton. I do not usually enjoy betting, but that evening I had a pocketful of expense account money and I played every match, and won. When we left I was over a hundred dollars ahead.

I went to the windows one more time to get large bills for my roll of singles when I saw Jaime, in blue, dressed as a security guard, with a large Magnum pistol tucked into a holster.

I went over to greet him and he seemed pleased and surprised to see me.

"When did you leave Nicaragua?" I asked.

"It was always only a matter of time," he explained with a shrug.

He grabbed his holster: "It's all right, I make a living, and I have my family with me," he added, as though anticipating all my questions, "and I sleep well enough, I suppose, but I am not really to be trusted here either."

I asked what he meant.

"This," he said, patting his holster, "It's only a replication."

"Replica?" I corrected him.

"Yes," he said, "is a fake. Solid bore. They give you this to scare people, but it don't work. No protection."

"That way nobody gets hurt," I pointed out.

"Maybe."

He seemed very glum. We exchanged addresses and phone numbers, though I knew I would probably not be calling him.

"This is some country," Jaime said. "They give you guns which don't shoot."

"I hope you find other work soon," I said.

"I do this for my wife and child," he told me.

Then he turned from me and walked away.

When Ortega initialed the Costa Rican peace proposal in Esquipulas, Guatemala, I called Jaime to congratulate him. A woman answered the phone, his wife. She said he left that morning for Managua. He felt it was safe to return and he hated working at the jaialai fronton. He was hoping the government would want him back.

Did I think that was likely? she asked me.

I didn't know and I told her so.

"Jaime never was a traitor," she said. "They must know that."

"Let's hope so," I said.

I asked if she would join him soon.

"It's better I stay here with the child," she said. "He may be coming back again in a big hurry."

It is a natural instinct in the majority of men to keep a secret garden in their souls, something that they do not care to talk about, still less to set down, for the other members of the herd to trample on.

Yesterday I received a letter from my friend in Managua:

"Time passes, and little by little, everything we have spoken in falsehood becomes true. It's a mistake to use a commuter ticket on the locomotive of history, and when I disembark the jungle crowds around me." ●

FROYLAN TURCIOS WAS A LONG TIME AGO (1987)

In San José, at the Pensión Costa Rica, the Chinese manager told me he'd put a letter under the door of my room.

All the rooms in this inexpensive lodging house were like monkish cells, separated by partitions that did not reach to the ceiling, though they all had doors which locked. I went down the first-floor corridor to my room and found the envelope, which was of linen paper and very white, with the engraved logo in black seriph script of a fancy Paris hotel.

Prudhomme wrote: "Glad I caught you at our old stopping place. You're well set up there, if you're short of cash. No sense in writing to you in Managua anyway, unless I wished our correspondence read by Nelida . . ."

Nelida, in this instance, was the FSLN's envoy to the press, the official censor. It was only after I had gotten this far in Prudhomme's letter that I was convinced by the handwriting, which was outsized and slanted backward, that he had acquired a mechanical hand.

He wrote: "It is not so bad being pampered by old wives and friends. I am writing an account of my time in the Chad in the form of a novel of espionage I call at this moment 'Under Benghazi.' Much has to be done to me and my truncated flesh before a prosthetic device can be attached (I hesitate to call it a hand) so I am learning to scrawl left-handed. This is one of the better results.

"I feel, as your mentor and guide, I owe you the following 'who's who' on Nicaraguan public life. Be guided by it, if you return:

"Ramirez, Sergio — *Hypocrite lecteur.*

"Borge, Tomás—Alleged castrato, he has kicked some men to death even as he was preparing to kneel and pray with them.

"Tirado, Victor—A member of the ruling 9 in charge of unions, who always says he has no power, being Mexican, especially when he is asked to intercede in a government act or policy with which he would rather not say he agrees.

"D'Escoto, Miguel—his papa was Somoza's bag man. He is Christ's, and, of course, the Sandies'.

"As you can see," Prudhomme went on, "my views are somewhat influenced by spleen. We Europeans still manage to be congenial regarding elites who disappoint us. Scoundrels abound, we mock them unsurprised. It is not that the other side in Miami, or Tegoo, are any less worthy of vilification? But they are perhaps better publicized. We know of the many former National Guard officers who serve the Contras. Do we know that Señor Ramirez once worked for the Somozas? I believe one must chew grape pits, as we say, in contemplating present-day Nicaraguan reality. A true anti-thug is in danger of being assassinated willy-nilly by either faction.

"Anyway, my dear friend, this is mainly to let you know that I continue to miss you more than I miss Nicaragua. Write or cable me at this address, but do not telephone, as I am never really here. Too many women wishing to console, so I've borrowed a cork-walled room in a flat nearby to practice elective silence which is necessary for scribble-scribble."

I was glad to hear from my friend, though put off by his maxims. Too often he spoke to me, or wrote to me, as though he were Madame De Sévigné instructing her daughter on the ways of society. I no longer felt like such a virgin, and though I appreciated his concern, felt much of it was displaced, misplaced. I, after all, still had two hands, and somewhat of a calling.

When I finished the two pages of the letter, I glanced across my small room in time to observe a tiny gray mouse on the washstand who was peering my way. The Chinese proprietors of the Pensión always were dousing the place with CN fumes and other anti-pest nostrums. This mouse was a true survivor. But I am one of those who find mice of any sort, in close proximity, utterly revolting, all sizes and colors, so I went out of the room to complain to the manager. He was not at the front desk. There was an open pack of Dentyne gum on the counter and I took a couple of segments to propitiate the gods of decay and, perhaps, ward off mouse-harm.

In the little conservatory and library next door, where we always took breakfast and read the papers, Sam Finer, the gold prospector, had just returned from another unprofitable expedition to the hills near Cartago and was glancing at *La Nación,* a dusty disheveled man with a deep tan and iron gray hair. San José is a city of exiles like Sam. The well-off buy villas or condos, or rent *apartotels.* Those without are in the pensions and boarding houses. Sam had been doing poorly in Costa Rica for quite some time, but he had prospects.

"I wish I knew as much about politics as I know about gold," he once said, glancing up ruefully, as was his custom.

"What do you know about gold?" I asked back. "You never find any."

"Not a booger's worth," Sam said.

From the hips up, Sam was well set up and sturdy, with a solid trunk, but he stood on little bandy legs like a punch-drunk boxer.

In the States, Sam had been quite well-to-do in "ladies' handbags," as he liked to put it. He'd made a bundle, retired, came to Costa Rica to open another small handbag factory with his only son, decided gold was far more lucrative. His son went off to Panama with a West Indian woman, and Sam was now on a reduced income as he panned for ore near the Central Valley.

He was, therefore, one of the regulars at the Pensión and he liked to talk a lot, always asking questions, so much so that I figured him for a "spook" at first, or someone Vesco left behind, until I realized he was just another gabby American, like so many other retirees in San José.

Finer had little gray wisps of hair on his brow above his eyes and they fluttered at me when he spoke: "Seems to me this war in Nicaragua has been going on so long it's getting boring."

"Only about a decade," I said. "And now they're talking peace, a cease fire."

"I'll believe it when it snows," Finer said. "Says here Sandino was fighting *gringos* in 1926."

He was holding up *La Nación,* which had a special feature on the anniversary of the death of the Honduran man of letters, Froylan Turcios, who had been Sandino's contact man with the "internationalists," as they were still called back then, until he left and went home to Honduras in despair. Turcios, it seemed, later died in exile in San José.

The newspaper writer put it: "Froylan Turcios was one of the most influential Hondurans of his era."

I said to Sam, "That's quite a thought, a Honduran of great influence."

"Sometimes you are a Yankee," Sam said.

"Well I never ran sweat shops in San José," I pointed out.

Sam corrected me: "We did embroidery. My women embroidered bags — no sweatshops — and I was encouraged by none other than Pepe Figueres."

His eyebrows moved at such a rapid pace I thought he might suddenly levitate from off his chair.

"Sorry," I said. "You know how I feel about Hondurans."

"You just don't like being bullied," Sam said.

I said, "Hondurans use Contras as a protection against disease."

"Not to worry," Sam said. "I use chewing gum. Where do you get the gum?"

I pointed over toward the desk.

"Incidentally," he added as he got up to go there, "This Froylan Turcios guy, what kind of a name was that?"

"Part Deutch, part Arab, I suspect, maybe Lebanese or Turco," I said, "to judge just from the name."

"You don't really know, do you?"

"That's correct," I replied.

"That's true of a lot of things we say and don't say," Sam said.

He bit his lower lip and then sat down again. "Well, anyway, sounds like one hell of a guy. They all do — Sandino too."

I said, "I once interviewed an old woman who remembered seeing Sandino when he came down to her village on horseback from his stronghold on the mountain, *El Chipote*. She says he was very small and sort of bow-legged."

"Is that all she remembered?" Sam asked.

"He came into her father's store to buy tobacco, and he bought this little girl, my informant, a boiled sweet."

"I once got patted on the head by Vice President Jack Garner," Sam said. "I must have been about twelve."

"It's not the same thing," I said.

"Why not?" Sam asked. "Why isn't it?"

"Because that's what politicians always do," I said. "It didn't cost him a cent."

"What you got against Americans?" Sam asked.

"Nothing."

"You're always knocking your own country, and chewing its gum," he said. "What a bitch."

"Would you be here if there weren't gold?" I asked.

"I like Latinos," he said. "They're so inefficient — and the Ticos are the most efficient of the inefficient so they don't get on your nerves. I like it here," he said. "I don't even really like chewing gum. I wear dentures."

Suddenly we were both laughing at each other, with easy amusement. Sam's glasses fell down low over the bridge of his nose. He said, finally, "Are you going back up to Nicaragua again?"

"Maybe," I said. "Maybe not."

Then I told him about Prudhomme, about his hand, and the letter I'd just received. He was nodding, as though he understood only too well. "That's pretty rough," Sam said. "You need a new buddy," he added. "Lonely enough down here. Must be even lonelier for you in Nicaragua without . . ."

"I often feel a little lost," I explained. "Even a con man like O. Henry felt lost down here."

Sam said, "Maybe you should go back home. It ain't your country and it ain't your struggle. Go to Israel maybe."

"I wouldn't feel any easier there," I said. "I feel much more at home down here. But I hate mice and the smell of disinfectant makes my sinuses raw."

"Same here," Sam said, "plus I got diverticulosis. When I get my nest egg back, maybe I'll move to Panama. By then I should be getting social security too. I'll buy a little bank."

"Sounds like more money than you'll ever see again from a pickaxe," I said.

"I'm a grandpa in Panama," Sam said. "I could come to see them with any number of little nuggets. Makes a big impression."

"Good as gold," I said.

"I wish I could get Medicare too, down here," Sam said, "but I eat a lot of bananas. Very soothing. The riper the better."

That's the way conversations go at the Pensión Costa Rica. Then they just trail off, as though they'd never commenced. Sam said, "If this country could figure out a way to make gasoline out of the banana." He never finished, but picked up his paper as though researching a new idea. Then he started talking about Europe in 1992 and how it would all be one big country with one currency and one army, and nobody in America was writing about that. I got up and went to my room for a cold shower.

That evening I left to see the movie *Ghostbusters,* in English with Spanish subtitles. Some theaters were showing it dubbed, but this audience was really having a ball with the English, and the funny cut-out costumes. So on.

In Morazón Park, on the way back, I thought a lot about ghosts. I never get scared, even when I feel haunted, but real life gives me the jitters. I made a special detour and stopped at the Soda Palace, opposite the Parque Central, for a cappuccino.

There were two Honduran kids at the next table. They'd just come from Managua; having witnessed the disasters of war they remained enthusiastic.

One of them, a smooth-faced boy with a large forehead, went on about "Nicaraguan Bonapartism," and the other, who was more Catholic, I suppose, and wore a large wooden cross between his pecs, nodded piously, as though supervising a catechism.

At last I interrupted to ask if they knew that today was the anniversary of the death of Froylan Turcios.

"Who he?" asked the speaker.

"Sandino's friend, " I said, "a great internationalist and man of letters."

"Oh, man," said the long-browed fellow in English, "that was such a long time ago —."

"Fifty years *mas o menos,*" I said.

"In fifty years I'll be dead," he said.

"If you're lucky," I said.

Scowling, he turned to his companion again.

I reached for some small bills to pay for my cappuccino.

It made me very sad to hear him call Turcios "a long time ago," even though I was just a tiny little kid in Turcios's era, because a lot of the same things were happening then as now. I figured in another generation they'd be saying stuff like that about this time in Central America, which is still with me — whenever I daydream, or fall asleep — like ghosts.

When I was little, my dad used to take me to Dodger games at Ebbets Field. We used to sit in his friend Abe Stark's box. Stark, a famous "clothier," had erected a big sign in right field. Any Dodger who hit Abe's sign with the ball got a free suit. I never saw it happen, though Abe always acted like a generous, benevolent man.

I thought he was a blowhard, like all my father's friends. I liked the Dodgers because they were not the Yankees. I sometimes think I like Central Americans for the same reason. I won a Cadillac in a raffle once, just after high school, and ran off to France to march in demonstrations against France's Vietnam War.

They don't even pretend to give away free suits anymore in Brooklyn, much less Central America. People get what they pay for with their corpses — and my father and his red-faced friends are all ghosts now.

Corpses everywhere, and so many new ghosts, too, and many new faces, hungry faces, demanding attention: The men of power always looking elsewhere. In Central America I've see almost as many one-armed men as I used to see in the mill towns of New England; and some are still hopeful, still dying for a fight, the final onslaught of blood, or dollars. Maybe they'll get lucky. The Yankees are inept, lazy. They have a plan, a program.

Maybe those kids at the Soda Palace would be lucky this time too, I thought, unlike Turcios and Sandino, and so many others who rose up, went underground, fell out, were betrayed or murdered. Maybe not. I knew I was not, which is why I was leaving Central America and the Soda Palace before I got hurt, like my friend Prudhomme.

As I was leaving the kid with the cross called out: "We saw you in *Ghostbusters.*"

I asked, "Was I laughing?"

"Very funny," said the other kid. "Junk food."

"I didn't like it that much," I pointed out.

"Transnational popcorn," the boy with the brow said.

I started toward the dark part of the street, with its broken pavements, to my little room without even a proper wall, in the reeky old Pensiōn Costa Rica.

That night I dreamed of baseball and bombs and ghosts. The departed are just like you and me except they have minds of their own and, when you want them to leave your dreams, they become all the more fixed and real, disappearing suddenly when you reach out to them in the darkness—and you wake up to the roar of traffic, the smell of diesel fumes, cars backfiring.

A new heart for a new man. One rule for travellers to Central America these days is any dream you enter you can always leave. The nights are dark to walk with doubtful feet.

December 1987●